TEACHERS' FAVORITES™

Fun Activities for

FALL!

Reproducible Patterns for Paper Crafts, Coloring Pages, Bookmarks, Decorations, and More!

Illustrations by George Hamblin

Publications International, Ltd.

Additional illustration by Shutterstock.

Introduction written by Holli Fort.

Sukodu puzzles by Howard Tomlinson.

Louis Weber, CEO
Publications International, Ltd.
7373 North Cicero Avenue
Lincolnwood, Illinois 60712

ISBN-13: 978-1-60553-984-3
ISBN-10: 1-60553-984-8

Manufactured in USA.

8 7 6 5 4 3 2 1

Contents

November 69

Fall into Fun Activities!

It's easy enough to color a turkey or draw a jack-o'-lantern. But having inventive and engaging activities that students respond to, have fun with, and maybe even learn from can be a daunting task, whether you lead a classroom, Sunday school class, scout troop, or a home filled with eager learners. The adaptable projects featured in *Teachers' Favorites*™: *Fun Activities for Fall!* will help you challenge your students with educational activities and purely fun seasonal projects that will delight them as they tap into their boundless creativity.

Each season offers up a unique buffet of holidays, milestones, sports, and activities. Fall is the time for Back to School, Halloween, Thanksgiving, colorful leaves, football, and pumpkins. Students will enjoy relevant crafts that can be hung, worn, read, laminated, given as gifts, or used to decorate the room or bulletin board.

Teachers' Favorites™: *Fun Activities for Fall!* includes the following types of activities:

- Coloring
- Games, such as word searches, connect the dots, and mazes
- Writing
- Counting
- Paper crafts

For craft projects, take the time to go over the instructions carefully. Also, make sure you have all the materials on hand before you get started. Here are just a few of the materials that are required for most projects:

Paper: Since the projects in this book will need to be photocopied, be sure to have plenty of paper. Most projects can be copied on regular copy paper, but some projects (such as paper dolls, cutouts that stand, etc.) should be copied on heavier stock or construction paper.

If you don't have access to heavier stock or your copier can't accommodate construction paper, you can glue the project to construction paper to make it sturdier. For some projects, such as cards, it is important that you not be able to see through the paper. In those cases, you may want to glue construction paper to the back of the paper to make the project work.

Glue and tape: Some projects call for glue and/or clear tape. Always use a water-base, nontoxic glue.

Scissors: Many projects call for cutting out pieces. Others require cutting slits or poking holes. For younger children, you may need to do the cutting yourself—or have older children help. Always have safety scissors on hand for smaller hands!

Brads: Some projects call for brass brads to hold pieces together. If you don't have those on hand, you can fashion them from twist ties.

Art supplies: Children can use crayons, markers, or paint to color these projects. If children will be painting, be aware that acrylic paint will dry permanently, though when wet it is easily cleaned up with water. Make sure children clean painting tools thoroughly when they are finished painting.

Art smock: Make sure children wear smocks or old shirts to protect clothes while working with paints and other messy materials.

Some children will be able to complete the crafts with little help, but there will be times when your assistance is needed. Other projects just need a watchful eye. So it's best if you review the project ahead of time and then make a decision about your role.

Flex Time

Another great thing about the crafts, coloring pages, and writing pages in this book is that they provide for versatility—which definitely comes in handy when working with children of

differing skill levels. The crafts can be simplified or made more complex depending on need.

Coloring pages are simple enough for younger children, but older children may want to challenge themselves by adding patterns, textures, or even decorations. Likewise, the writing pages are great for older children to let their imaginations flow in creating original stories, while beginning writers may use them to copy a few words or dictate longer stories to an adult. If your group is of mixed ages, consider taking a teamwork approach that combines the imaginative approach of a younger child and the writing skills of an older child.

Great Clips

Clip art pages are great for all kinds of applications. You can use a copy machine to increase the size of the seasonal images to make them suitable for wall or bulletin board decorations. (Use an overhead or opaque projector to create very large images.) Likewise, you can use the copier to make images smaller for use on worksheets, bulletins, notes to parents, or any other application you can dream up. Incorporate the clip art images to create seasonal birthday cards or stationery, or just use them to add a decorative element to any other project.

In the Mix

All of the projects presented in this book, from the simplest to the most elaborate, are just ideas to get you started crafting. Feel free to play around with the designs, choosing different materials or embellishing in any number of unique ways. Give your imagination free rein as you play around with materials and these base ideas. Encourage students to come up with their own unique variations on these themes, and keep them in mind for later uses. You can jump off in any direction, keeping these projects as fun and fresh as the first time you tried them. When it comes to creating fun fall activities, the sky is the limit!

Back-to-School Time!

Fall Fun!

Crown Birthday Royalty

Color the crown, then cut it out. Have an adult help you glue or tape the pieces together so it fits around your head. Have a royally wonderful birthday!

It's Labor Day!

In September, we celebrate all the hard work people do. What job do you want when you grow up? Color all the uniforms and a paper doll so it looks like you, and cut them all out. Then try each uniform on your doll. There is an empty uniform for you to draw your own clothing if you'd like to be something we have not drawn for you.

How I Spent My Summer

Write a story about an exciting adventure you had this summer.

_____

_____

_____

_____

_____

_____

_____

_____

_____

Crazy Classroom

Can you find these seven items hidden in the classroom?

Answers on page 95.

Alphabet Letter Fun

Color these fun bubble letters and the objects next to them that start with that letter. If there is no object next to a letter, can you draw something next to it that begins with that letter?

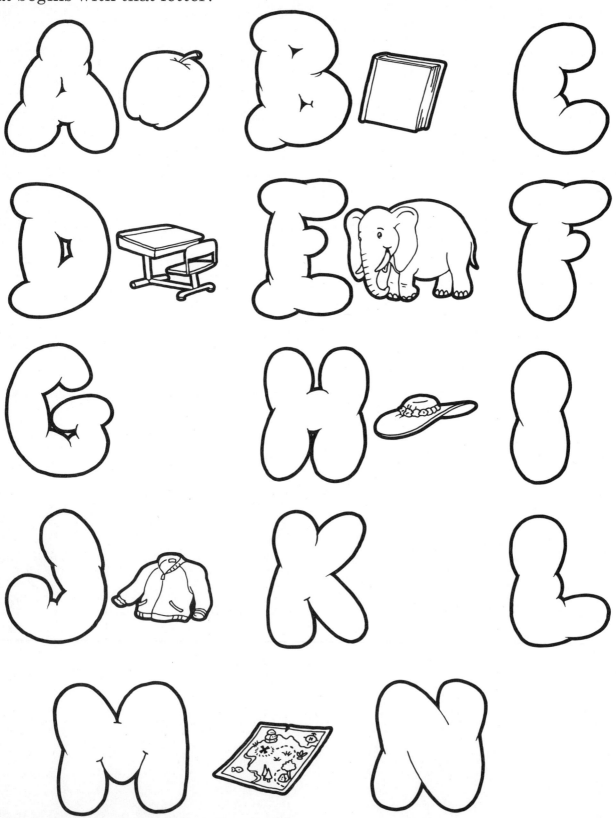

Grandparents Are the Best!

Grandparents Day is celebrated the first Sunday after Labor Day. Color the card on the next page and the objects on this page. Cut them all out, and fold the card in half. Write a special message to your grandparents or someone special in your life. Glue or tape the objects to the card to decorate it.

Family Tree

Fill in this family tree with all your family's information, including names and birth dates. Call your grandparents, and ask them about their lives when they were kids, or ask your parents about their childhoods. We bet you'll hear some interesting stories!

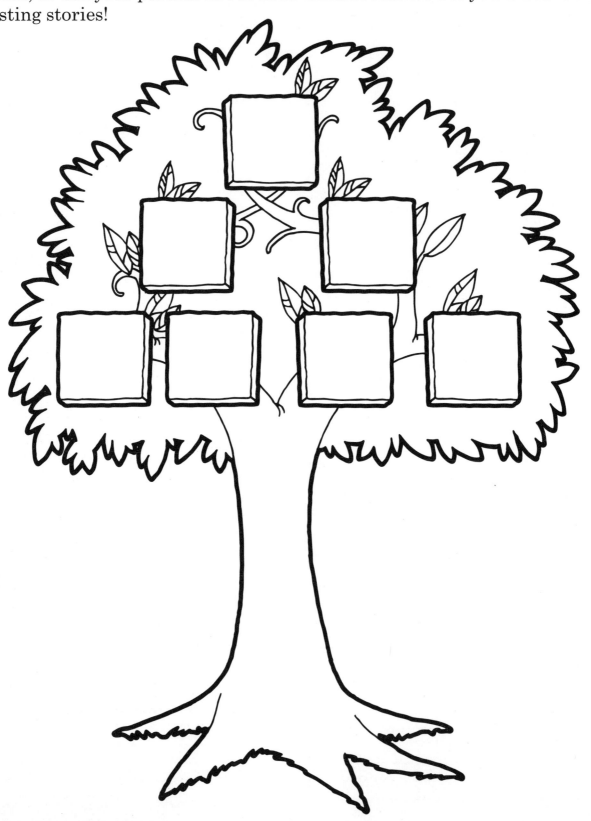

My Family

Use the outlines to draw in your family. Be sure to include your grandparents!

Let's Go to the Library!

September is Library Card Sign-up Month. Make sure you get your library card soon. Have fun coloring these kids using their library cards!

. . . . **Let's Go to the Library!** . . . .

Bookmarks Mark the Spots!

Make bookmarks for your library books! Draw your own design on the blank bookmark. Color, cut out, and add ribbon or yarn.

School's In

Look at the pictures on this page, and name each one. They all are things you'd find in a classroom. Write each word in the correct numbered spaces.

Across

1.

5.

6.

Down

2.

3.

4.

Answers on page 95.

How Many Apples?

Can you count all the apples on this page? Then color the picture.

Answer on page 95.

Ahoy, Me Matey!

September 19 is International Talk Like a Pirate Day. Color these pirate kids!

Be a Pirate!

Color and cut out your eye patch, and have an adult help you add string so you can wear it. Color and cut out your own pirate parrot, too!

Football Fun!

Fall is football time! Color and cut out the figures. Use the stands to make them stand up. Color the field, place the goal posts, and have a friend use his or her team to play a game.

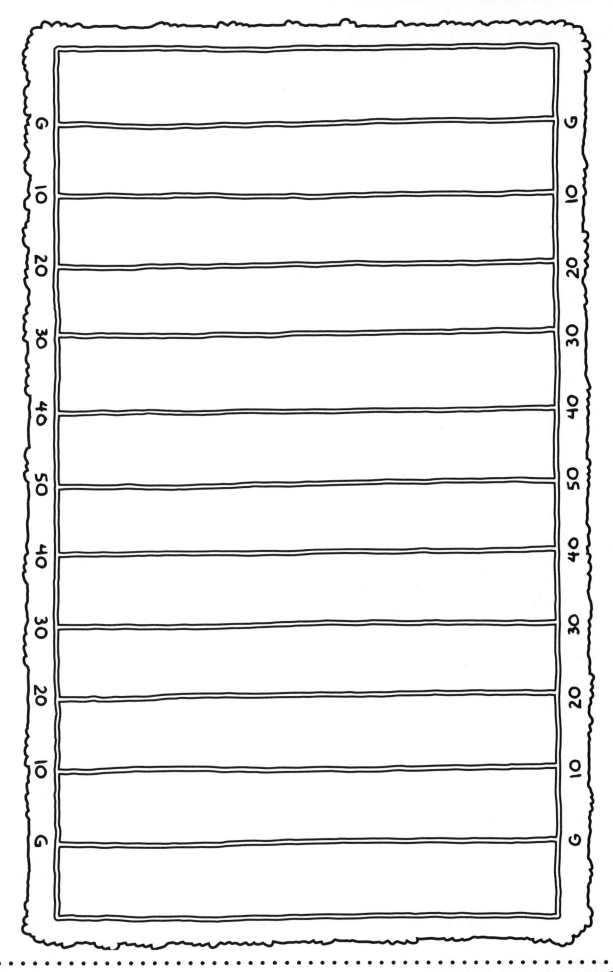

Apple Memory Game

Let's play a game! First, though, you'll need to glue construction paper to the back of the cards. Then color the card fronts, and cut the cards out. Now it's time to play! Turn all the cards over (showing the construction paper side), and everyone takes a try by turning over two cards to find a match. Concentrate!

An Apple a Day

Help this hungry worm make it through this tasty treat!

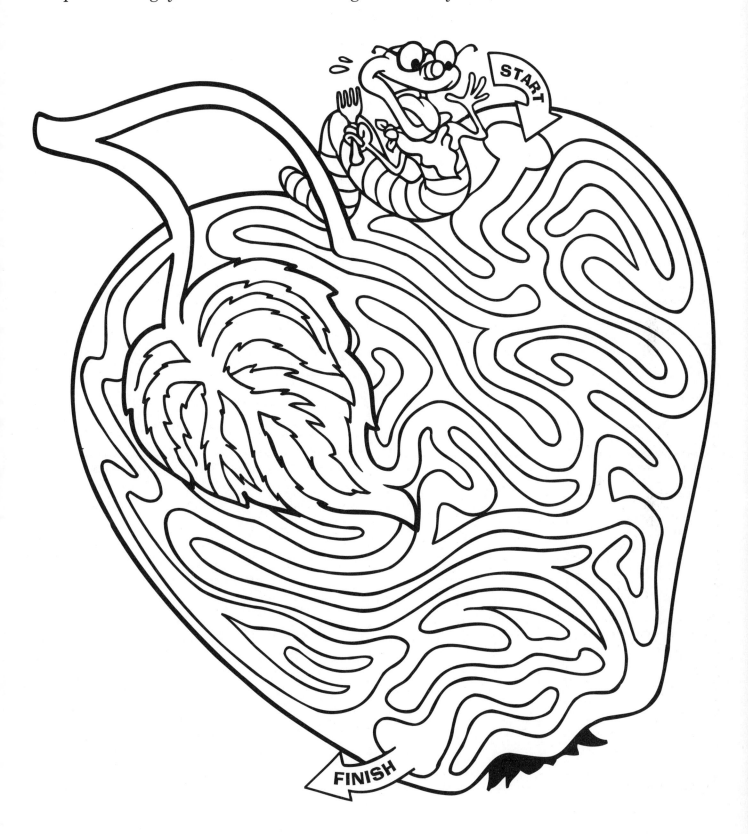

Answer on page 95.

Bird Migration Mania!

In the fall, when the weather starts getting colder, many birds travel south to warmer places. This is called migration. Color the birds and wings, and cut them out. Have an adult help you cut the wing slit, and insert the wings into the birds' bodies. Now it's time to play a migration game. Grab a big bowl or pail, and head outside. Take turns "flying" your birds into the bowl. Whoever gets the most in the bowl wins Migration Mania!

Sharp-Eyed Spotter

Only two of these pictures are the same. Can you spot the matching pair?

Answer on page 95.

The Leaves Are Falling!

Write about your favorite fall activities.

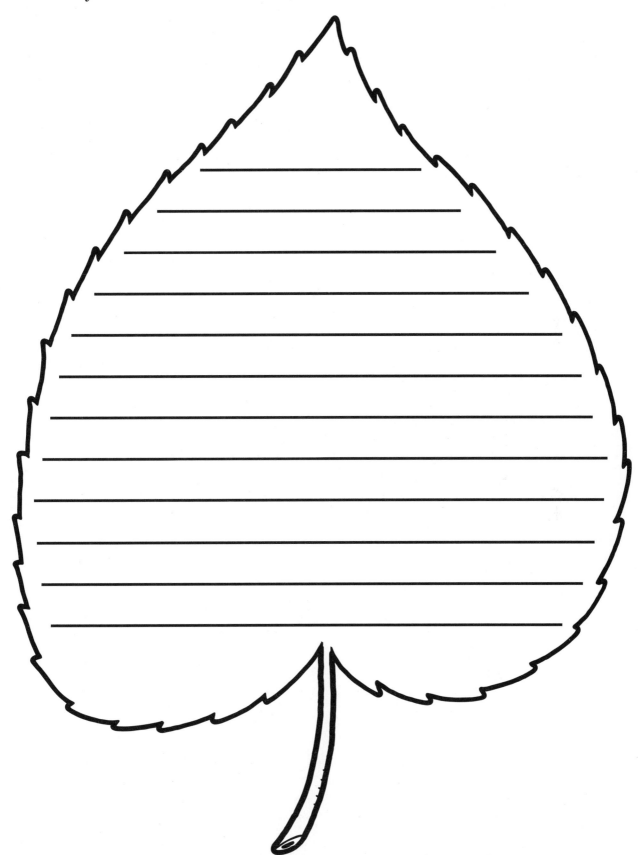

Leaves, Leaves, and More Leaves!

Can you identify these leaves?

1.

2.

3.

4.

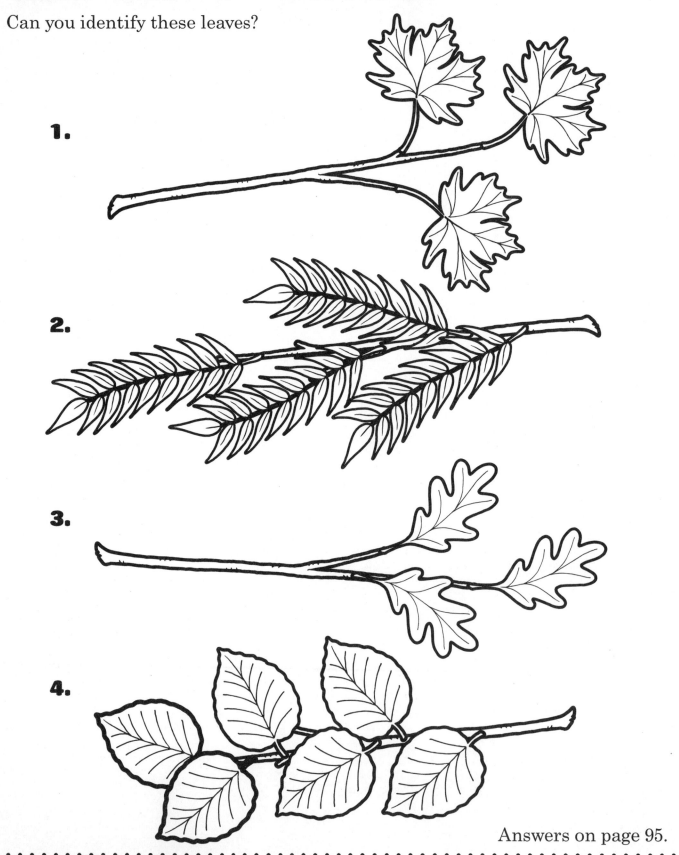

Answers on page 95.

Raking Up the Fun!

Color these kids who just couldn't say no to jumping into that big pile of leaves!

October Fun!

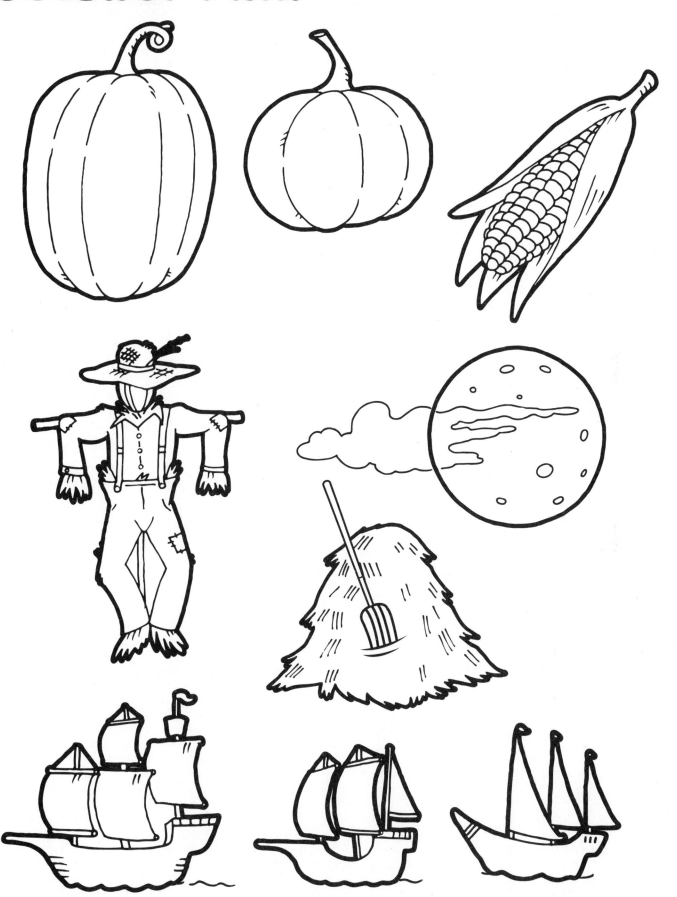

Boo Time!

Birthday Bling

Color and cut out the cake and stars. String them on yarn or ribbon, and put on your birthday bling to celebrate your special day!

October Poetry

Write a poem about your favorite October happenings!

_____

_____

_____

_____

_____

_____

_____

_____

Unfurl Your Flag for Columbus Day!

Christopher Columbus discovered America in 1492. This is the flag he flew on his ships. Color his flag, then design your own flag!

Columbus Discovers America

Columbus sailed three ships to America: the Niña, the Pinta, and the Santa Maria. Have fun coloring this scene!

Haunted House Maze

You're trapped on the roof of a haunted house, and you have to find your way through the house and out the front door. Use ladders and doorways to help you escape. Watch where you're going. Some rooms and stairs lead to dead ends—or worse!

Answer on page 95.

World Space Week

Celebrate the exploration of space in October with World Space Week. Now you can pretend to explore other planets! Color, cut out, and play with these astronauts, space shuttle, and land rover.

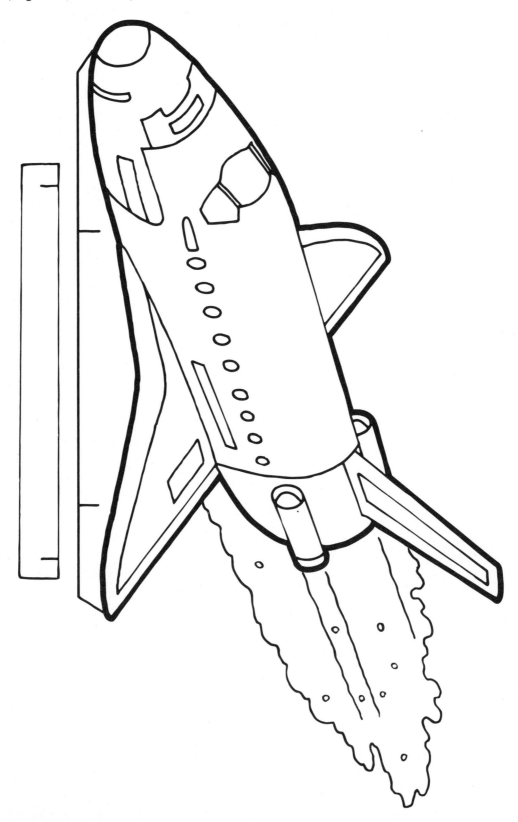

Take a Whirl Around the Solar System

Make a mobile of our solar system. Color and cut out the planets and the sun. Hang the planets from the sun with string.

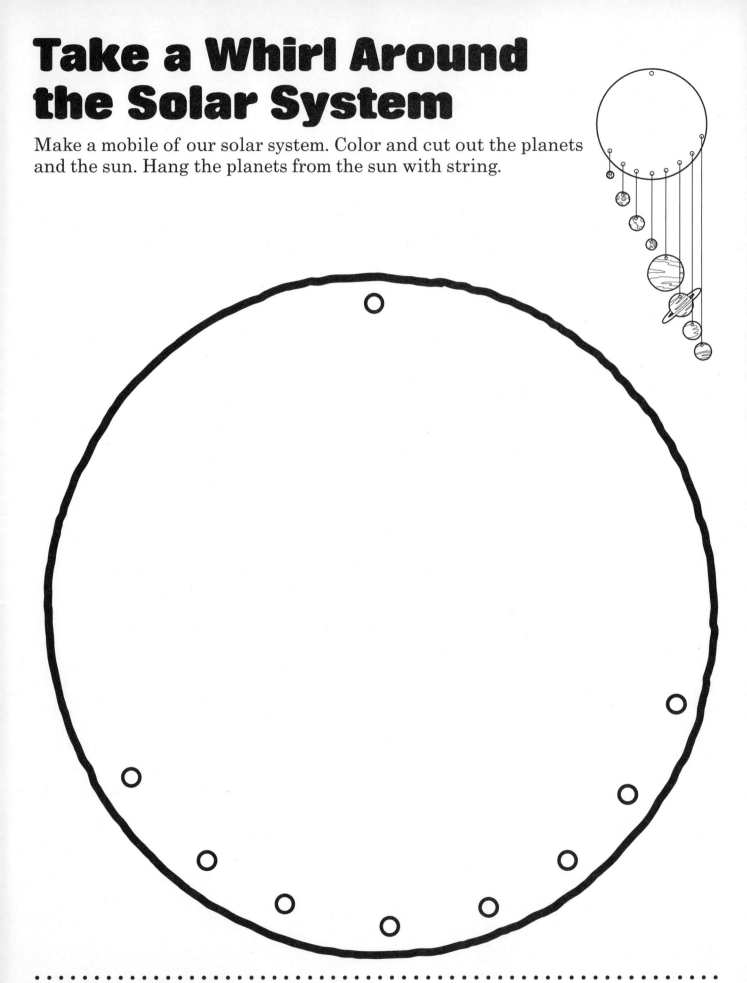

Neptune

Uranus

Saturn

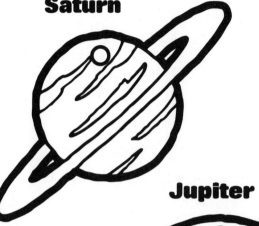

Jupiter

Mars

Earth

Venus

Mercury

Fred's Tips for Fire Safety!

Fire Safety Week is in October. Fred the Firefighter wants to give kids some safety tips. Color Fred, write some safety tips, and hang him in your home to remind everyone in your family what to do in case of an emergency.

Fire Engine to the Rescue!

The fire engine is almost ready to help out at the next fire. Can you complete this one so the firefighters can get to work? Color and cut out the truck and wheels. Use brads or glue to attach the wheels, fold the truck to create a box, and you're ready to race to the fire!

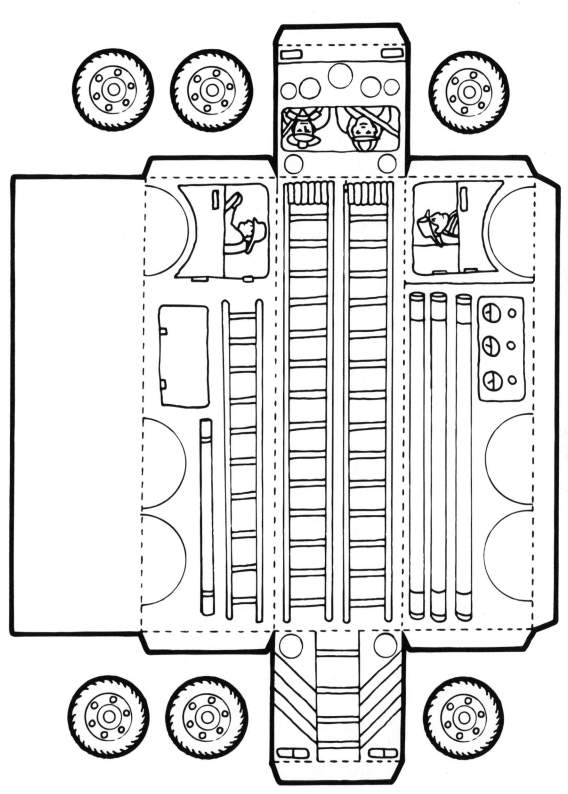

Universal Children's Week

It's time to celebrate all the children of the world! Color these children dressed in the clothes of their homelands, and be sure to color yourself in the last child! Cut out all the children, and glue or tape their hands together so they form a ring to show we are all connected—all part of the same world!

Worldwide Pen Pal

Write a letter to a child in another country. Tell them about your life, and ask them what life in their homeland is like. Don't forget to color the flags of the world!

Dear _____,

_____

_____

_____

_____

_____

_____

_____

_____

_____

Bewitching

Read each sentence. If it's true, circle the letter in the True column. If it's false, circle the letter in the False column. Then read the circled letters from top to bottom to find the answer to this riddle: What is a witch's favorite school subject?

	True	False
An apple is a fruit.	S	T
Shoes go on your hands.	N	P
A dime equals ten pennies.	E	A
A toothbrush is for your hair.	O	L
The president lives in an igloo.	H	L
Tricycles have three wheels.	I	F
A lion has four legs.	N	W
Jack-o'-lanterns are for Easter.	S	G

Answer on page 95.

Halloween Masks

Color and cut out these fun Halloween masks. Don't forget to cut out the eyeholes! Have an adult help you attach ribbon or string to tie the mask to your head.

Skelly the Skeleton

Cut out Skelly, and use brads or twist ties to attach the parts of his skeleton. Hang him up for some bony fun!

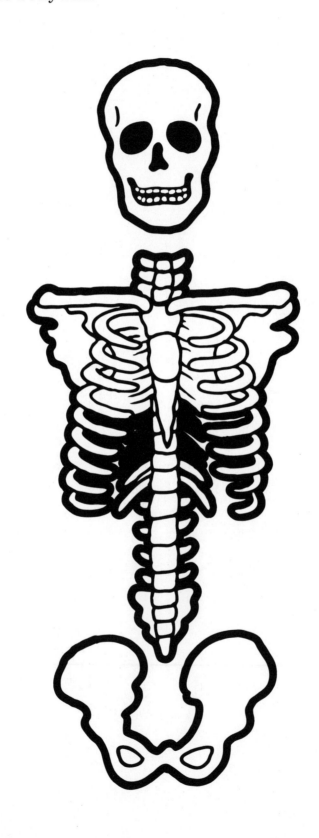

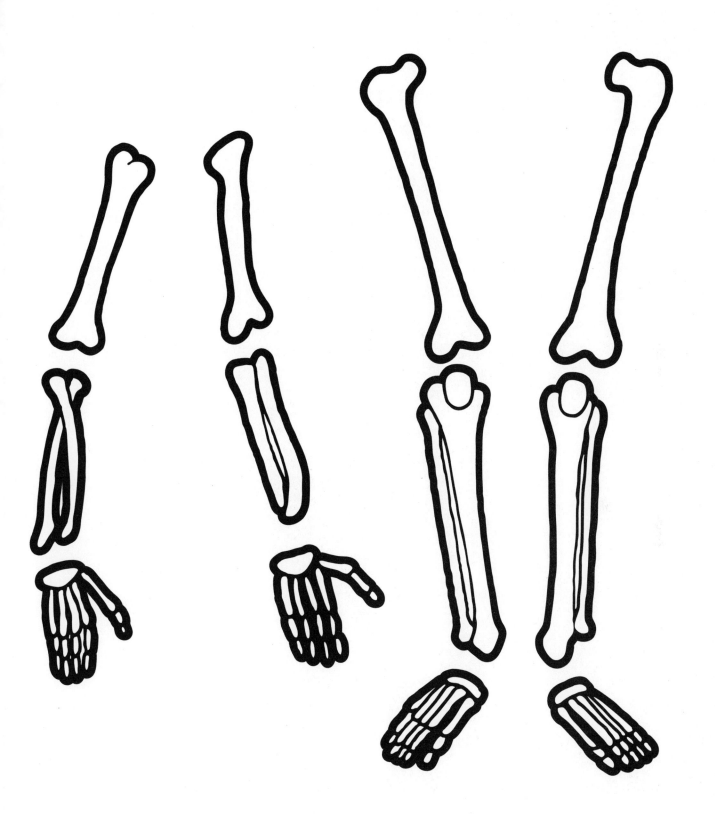

Happy Halloween

Circle the ten words about Halloween that are hidden in the jack-o'-lantern. Words may run forward or backward, up or down, or along diagonals, but they are always in a straight line.

Word list

COSTUME
GHOST
MASK
OCTOBER
OWL
PUMPKIN
SKELETON
TREAT
TRICK
WITCH

```
                    G

         J  E  O  U  H  C  O

      C  W  I  T  C  H  O  S  D

   U  O  P     M  V  T     S  Y  X

   Q  S  K  E  L  E  T  O  N  T  W

   M  T  P  C  J     G  W  B  R  E

   P  U  M  P  K  I  N  L  I  E  M

   O  M     C     Z     M     A  R

      E  B                 S  T

         E  T  R  I  C  K  T
```

Answers on page 96.

Jack-o'-Lanterns

Draw silly faces on these pumpkins!

Halloween Pop-up Card Tricks

Make a *spook*-tacular pop-up card for your favorite ghost or ghoul! Have an adult help you fold on the dashed lines and cut the solid lines, then glue the card (but not the tabs that are cut!) to construction paper. Color the figures on this page. Fold the card in half, with the white card on the inside and the tabs folded out. Open the card, and glue figures to the tabs. Then write a Halloween greeting on the card front. Use the leftover figures to decorate the rest of your card!

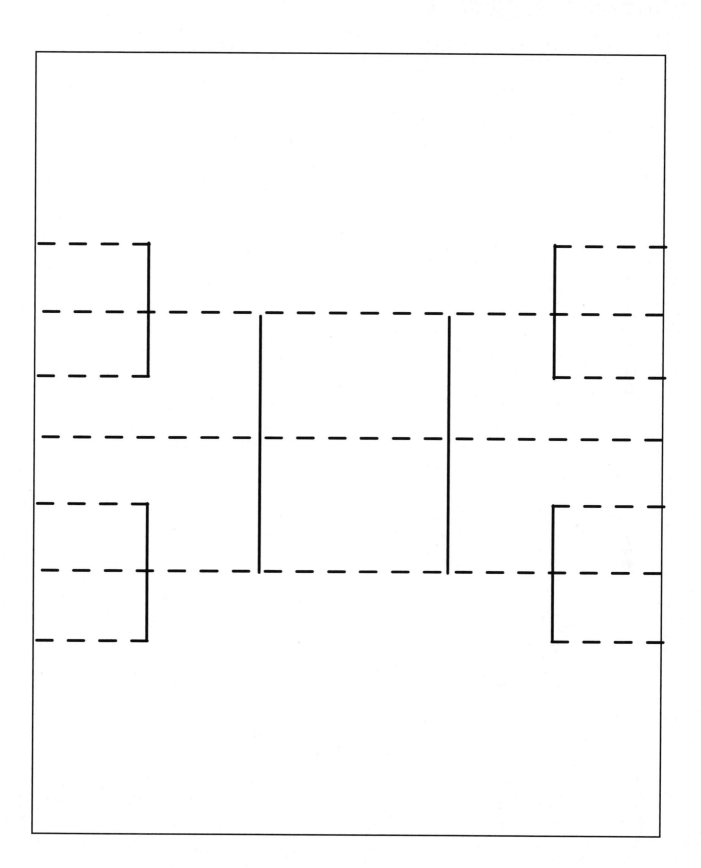

It's Bingo Time!

Color your bingo cards and each of the bingo pieces. Glue the pieces to a piece of construction paper so the design won't show through to the back, and cut them out. It's time to play bingo! Give everyone a card, and use buttons, beans, or pennies to mark the place on your card as each bingo piece is called. First one to get three in a row or four anywhere on their card wins!

Halloween Storytelling

We've started a spooky story for you—now you get to finish it. Your story can be scary, silly, or just fun. Be sure to color the scene so that your page is *boo*-tiful!

It was a dark and stormy night, _____

_____

_____

_____

_____

_____

_____

_____

_____

Take Me to Your Mummy

He's tricked or treated, and now he can't get out of his costume! Help this mummy unravel his wrappings so he can dig into his candy.

Answer on page 96.

November Fun!

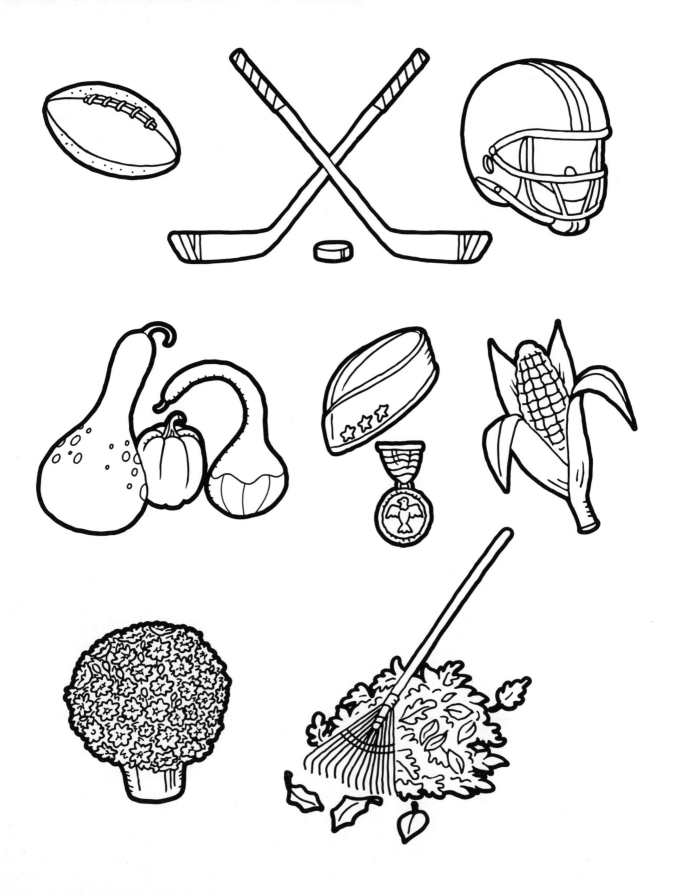

Thanksgiving Decorations

You're the Birthday Star Today!

If it's your birthday, color and cut out the star. Write your name on the star. Have an adult pin it to your shirt with a safety pin. Then let everyone celebrate with you!

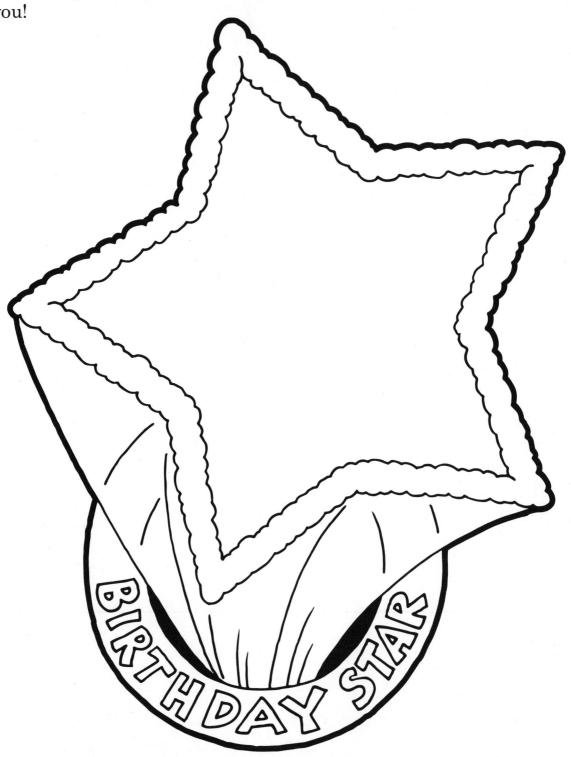

BIRTHDAY STAR

November Writing Page

Write a story about your favorite November activity.

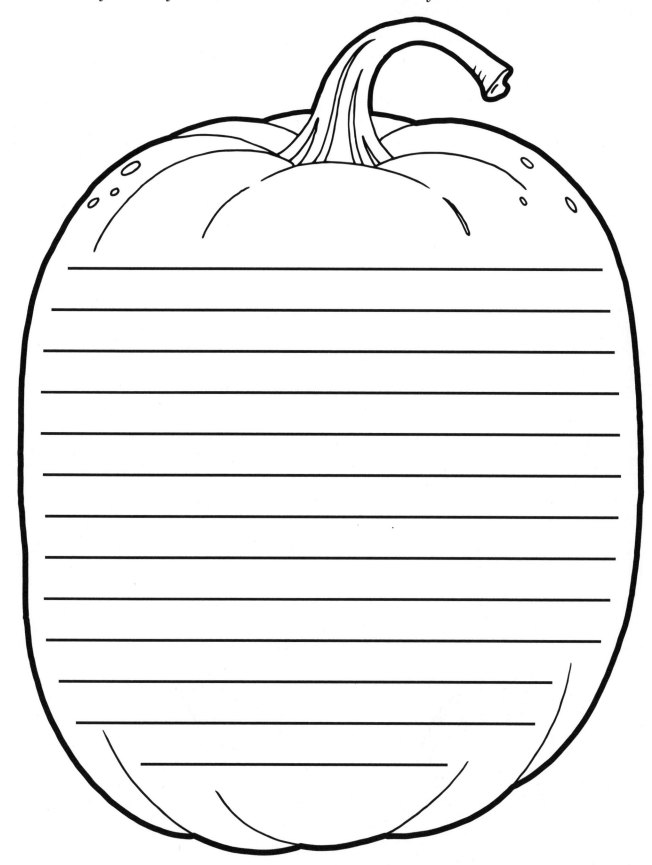

Hooray for Aviation!

November is National Aviation Month, so let's fly! Color and cut out the helicopter, and attach the rotor with a brad. It's time to take off for the wild blue yonder!

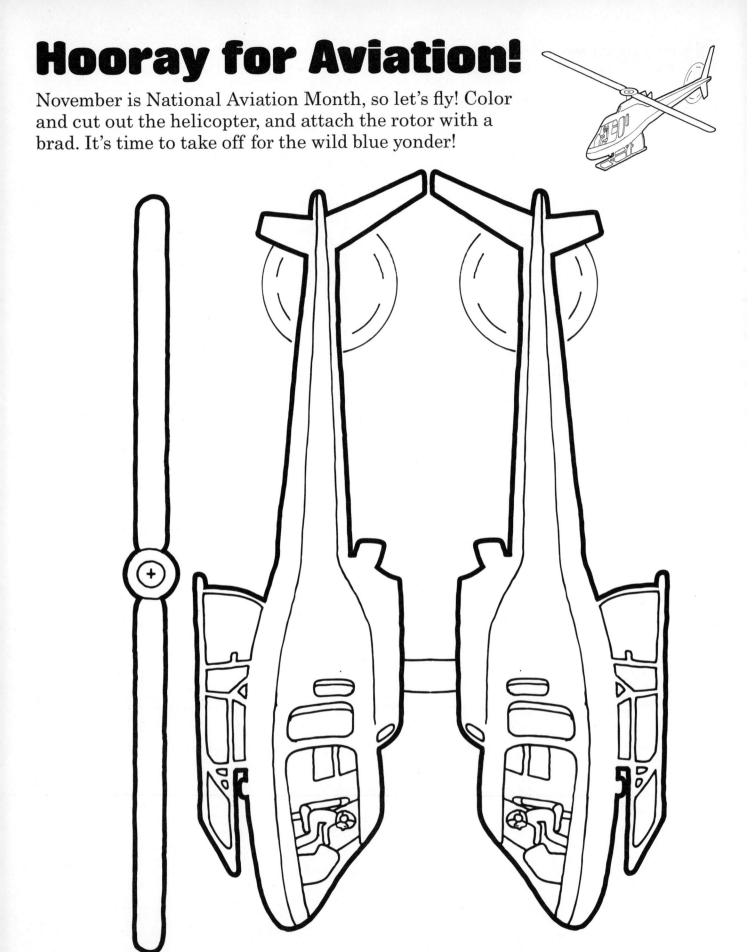

Humane Society Anniversary

Celebrate the Humane Society by coloring this boy and girl helping out at an animal shelter.

Save Our Planet!

November 15 is America Recycles Day! Can you find the five problems with this household?

Answers on page 96.

Recycling for Art and Fun!

Color all the insect wings, eyes, and antennae, and cut them out. Cut cups from washed and dried egg cartons, and glue on the pieces to create fun bugs!

Veterans Day

Who doesn't love a parade, especially when it honors the soldiers who have fought so bravely for our country!

Honor Your Heroes

Color these medals, and cut them out. Then give one to each of your heroes!

November Is Fun Month!

National Game and Puzzle Week falls in November, so on the next few pages we've come up with some great puzzles and games for you!

Sudoku

This puzzle is all about logic. Only one of each Thanksgiving symbol can be in each 6×2 box, row, and column. Cut out the symbols, and use them to solve the puzzles!

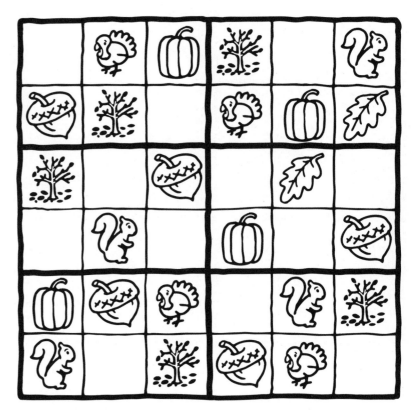

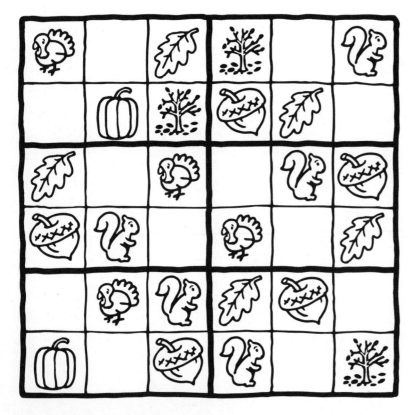

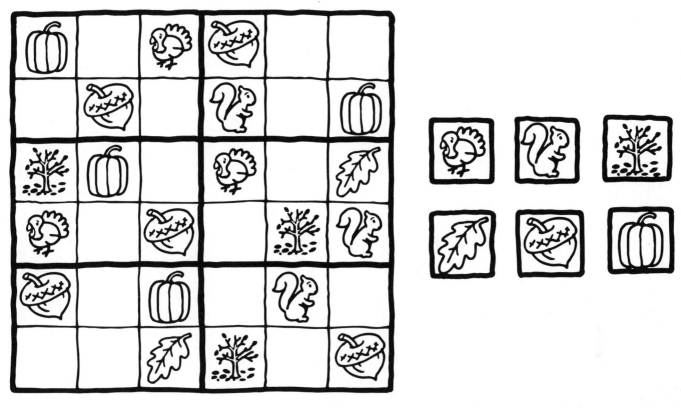

Answers on page 96.

Fun Activities for Fall! 81

What Am I?

Connect the dots to find a favorite November animal.

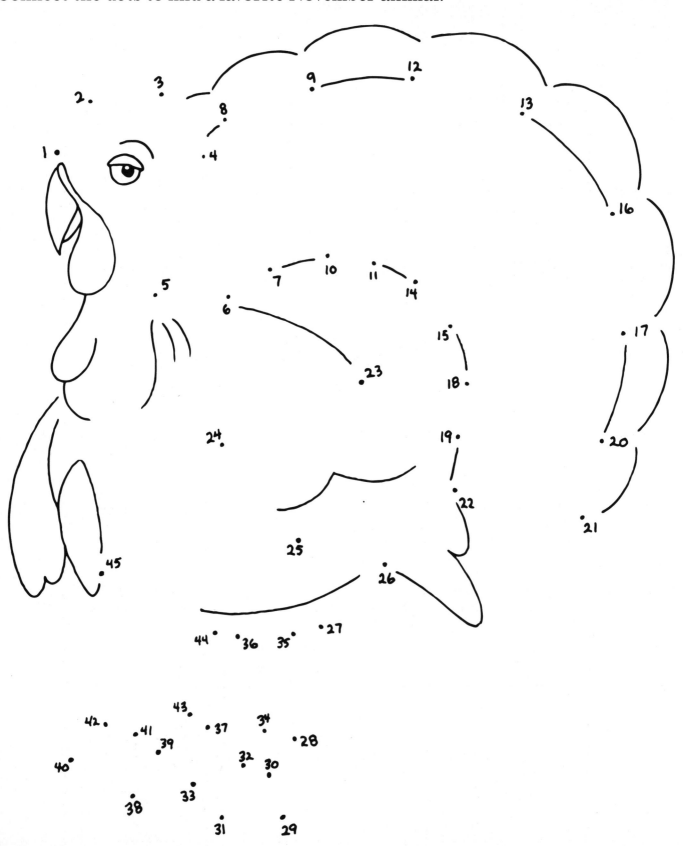

Thanksgiving Feast Match-Up

This game is played just like Go Fish. Keep playing until all the Thanksgiving meal dishes are gone!

Note to teacher: Make 2 copies of page for each student.

Author, Author!

National Author's Day, I Love to Write Day, and National American Teddy Bear Day are all in November. So write your own story about your favorite teddy bear in this mini book. Color the cover, cut out the pages, and glue or staple the pages inside the cover. Congratulations, you're an author!

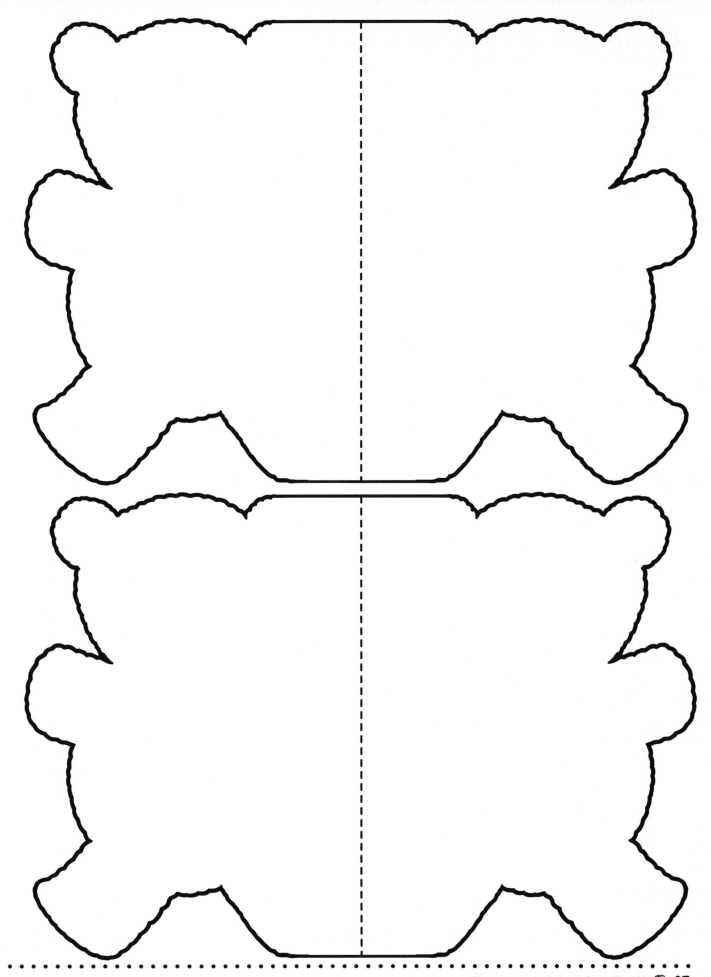

Thanksgiving Day Table Place Cards

Help decorate your Thanksgiving dinner table! Make a place card for everyone. Color the figures and cards. Write a name on each card, and fold the cards in half. Glue a figure to each card, and place them on the table to show everyone where they will be sitting.

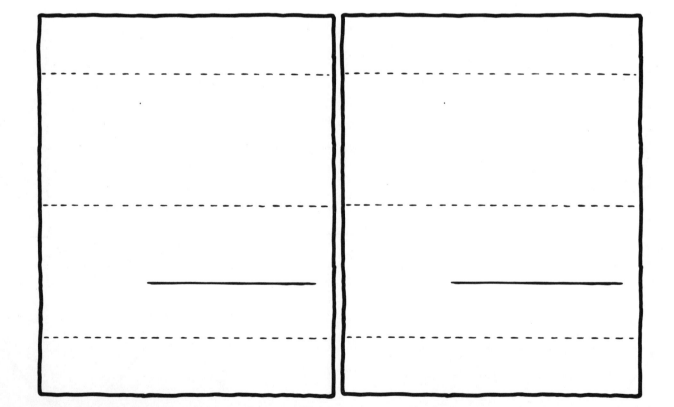

Thanksgiving Placemat

Make a special placemat for your Thanksgiving dinner! Color and cut it out.
Have an adult laminate it for you so it lasts for a long time.

What I'm Thankful For

Thanksgiving Writing Page

Write about all the things you're thankful for this year. For a special
Thanksgiving treat, read it to everyone at the dinner table.

_____

_____

_____

_____

_____

_____

_____

_____

_____

Thanksgiving Finger Puppets

When dinner is over, it's time for puppet theater! Color and cut out the puppets, tape or glue the other pieces to the strip, and tape the strip around your finger. Then write your own script, and entertain your whole family!

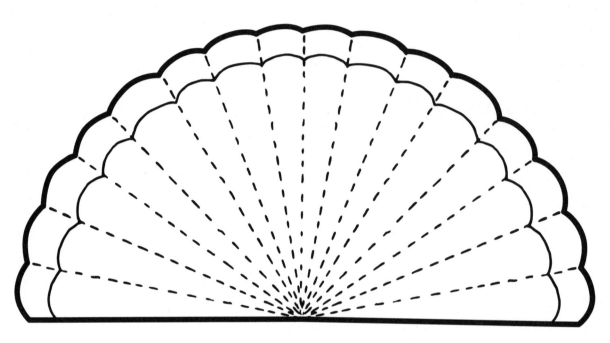

Give Thanks Box

Color and cut out the box pattern. Fold the pattern into a box, and tape it. Then cut out the slips. Before Thanksgiving dinner, hand out slips to everyone and ask them to write what they are thankful for. Then have everyone put the slips into the box, and after dinner everyone can pull a slip and read it. It will remind everyone of all of life's blessings!

I'm thankful for
_____

I'm thankful for
_____

I'm thankful for
_____

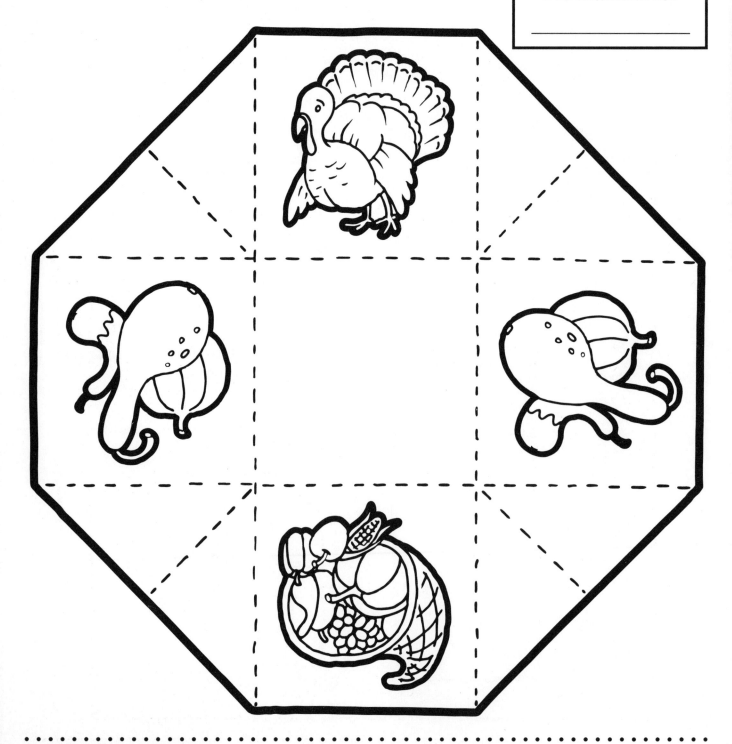

I'm thankful for

Thanksgiving Frame

Color the frame, then cut it out, including the center. Have an adult help you cut cardboard the same size for backing. Place a picture of someone you're thankful for in the hole facing out, and glue the frame to the cardboard.

National Tongue Twister Day

Everyone loves a tongue twister! Practice saying this twister, then write your own in the shapes provided.

Peter Piper picked a peck of pickled peppers.

If Peter Piper picked a peck of pickled peppers,

where's the peck of pickled peppers Peter Piper picked?

Answers

Crazy Classroom (page 15)

School's In (page 24)

A	P	P	L	E			D
E				G			E
N				L			S
C			B	O	O	K	
I				B			
G	L	A	S	S	E	S	

How Many Apples? (page 25)
There are 25 apples.

An Apple a Day (page 31)

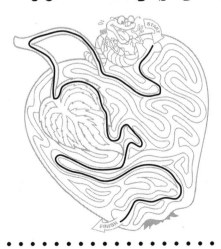

Sharp-Eyed Spotter (page 34)

Leaves, Leaves, and More Leaves (page 36)

1. maple; 2. ash; 3. oak; 4. basswood

Haunted House Maze (page 45)

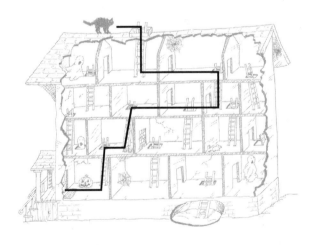

Bewitching (page 54)
SPELLING

Happy Halloween *(page 60)*

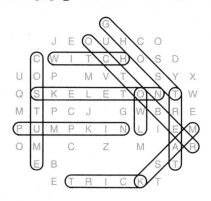

Take Me to Your Mummy
(page 68)

Save Our Planet! *(page 76)*

1. Water running; 2. no one in room but TV on; 3. refrigerator door open; 4. recyclables in trash; 5. car running but Dad going back in house

November Is Fun Month!
(pages 80–81)

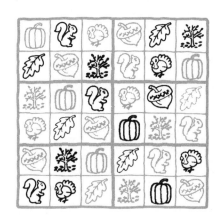

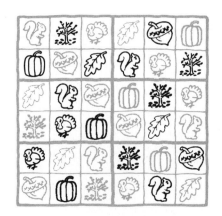

TEACHERS' FAVORITES™

Fun Activities for
WINTER!

Reproducible Patterns for
Paper Crafts, Coloring Pages, Games,
Decorations, and More!

Illustrations by George Hamblin

Publications International, Ltd.

Introduction written by Holli Fort.

Louis Weber, CEO
Publications International, Ltd.
7373 North Cicero Avenue
Lincolnwood, Illinois 60712

ISBN-13: 978-1-60553-983-6
ISBN-10: 1-60553-983-X

Manufactured in USA.

8 7 6 5 4 3 2 1

Table of Contents

Heat Things Up with Winter Craft Fun!

It's easy enough to color a reindeer or cut out a snowman. But having inventive and engaging activities that students respond to, have fun with, and maybe even learn from can be a daunting task. This is true whether you lead a classroom, Sunday school class, scout troop, or a home filled with eager learners. The adaptable projects featured in *Teachers' Favorites*™*: Fun Activities for Winter!* will help you challenge your students with educational activities and purely fun seasonal projects.

Each season in this four-book series offers up a unique buffet of holidays, milestones, sports, and activities. Winter is the time for Christmas, Hanukkah, Kwanzaa, Valentine's Day, ice hockey, and playing in the snow. Students will enjoy relevant crafts that can be hung, worn, read, laminated, given as gifts, or used to decorate the room or bulletin board.

Teachers' Favorites™*: Fun Activities for Winter!* includes the following types of activities:

• Coloring

• Writing

• Math

• Paper crafts

• Games, such as look-and-find, connect the dots, and mazes

For craft projects, take the time to go over the instructions carefully. Also, make sure you have all the materials on hand before you get started. Here are just a few of the materials that are required for most projects:

Paper: Since the projects in this book will need to be photocopied for each student, be sure to have plenty of paper. Most projects can be copied on regular copy paper, but some projects (such as paper dolls and cutouts that stand) should be copied on heavier stock or construction paper. If you do not have access to heavier stock or your copier cannot accommodate construction paper, you can glue the project's paper to construction paper to make it sturdier. For some projects, such as the holiday card, it is important that you can't see through the paper. In such cases, you might want to glue construction paper to the back of the paper.

Glue and tape: Some projects call for glue and/or clear tape. If you use glue, make sure it is water-base and nontoxic.

Scissors: Many projects call for cutting out pieces. Some require cutting slits or poking holes. For younger children, you may need to do the cutting yourself—or have older children help. Always have safety scissors around for smaller hands!

Brads: Some projects call for brass brads to hold pieces together. If you do not have those on hand, you can substitute brads with twist ties.

Art supplies: Children can use crayons, markers, or paint to color these projects. If children will be painting, be aware that acrylic paint will dry permanently, though when wet it is easily cleaned up with water. Make sure children clean painting tools thoroughly when they are finished painting.

Art smock: Make sure children wear smocks or old shirts to protect clothes while working with paints and other messy materials.

Flex Time

Another great thing about the crafts, coloring pages, and writing pages in this book is that they provide for versatility—which definitely comes in handy when working with children of differing skill levels. The crafts can be simplified or made more complex depending on need.

Coloring pages are simple enough for younger children, but older children may want to challenge themselves by adding patterns, textures, or even decorations. Likewise, the writing pages are great for older children to let their imaginations flow in creating original stories, while beginning writers may use them to copy a few words or dictate longer stories to an adult to write for them. If your group is of mixed ages, consider taking a teamwork approach that combines the imaginative approach of a younger child and the writing skills of an older child.

Great Clips

Clip-art pages are great for all kinds of applications. You can use a copy machine to increase the size of the seasonal images to make them suitable for wall or bulletin board decorations. Likewise, you can use the copier to make images smaller for use on worksheets, bulletins, notes to parents, or any other application you can dream up. Incorporate the clip-art images to create seasonal birthday cards or stationery, or use them to add a decorative element to any other project.

In the Mix

All of the projects presented in this book, from the simplest to the most elaborate, are just ideas to get you started. Feel free to alter the designs by choosing different materials or embellishing in any number of unique ways. Give your imagination free rein as you play around with materials and these base ideas. Encourage students to come up with their own unique variations on these themes, and keep them in mind for later uses. You can jump off in any direction, keeping these projects as fun and fresh as the first time you tried them. When it comes to creating fun wintertime activities, the sky is the limit!

Winter Fun!

December Holidays

A Birthday Gift

Celebrate this month's birthdays with this fun gift box. Color, cut out, and write your name in the space.

Build a Snowman!

This snowman needs help! Can you put him back together again? Color and cut out all of the pieces of the snowman, then arrange them. You can also paste the snowman to a piece of construction paper once you sort things out!

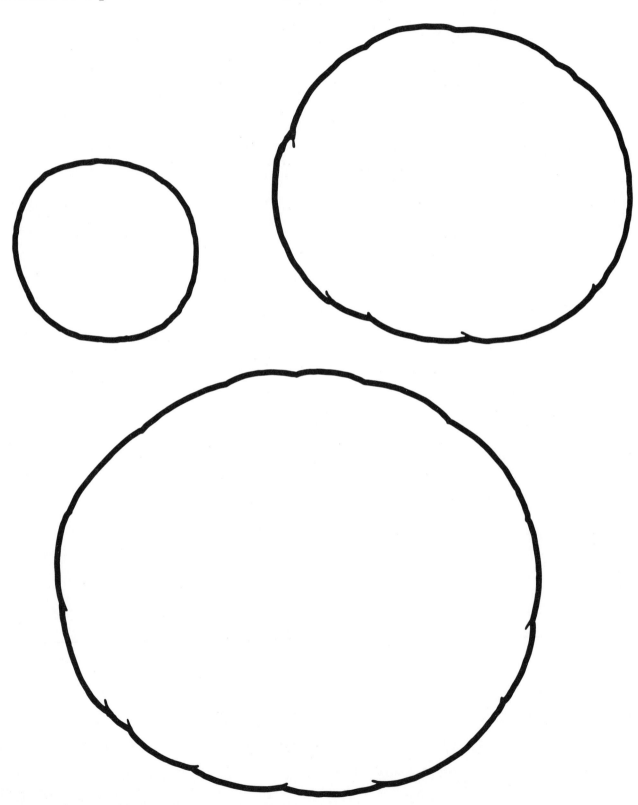

School Days

Pull out your crayons or markers. Color the circles yellow, the squares blue, the triangles red, and the rectangles green. Fill in the rest of the scene with whatever colors you want.

Winter Outdoor Fun!

Do you like to play outside when it's cold and snowy? Draw yourself doing something fun you like to do outside in the winter. You can also draw yourself trying something new that you've never done before!

Bundle Up!

When you go outside in the winter, you have to make sure that you wear lots of warm clothes. Can you help this boy and girl get dressed so they can go play outside? Color the boy and girl and all of their clothes. Cut everything out, and then put the clothes on the dolls. Try on lots of different outfits!

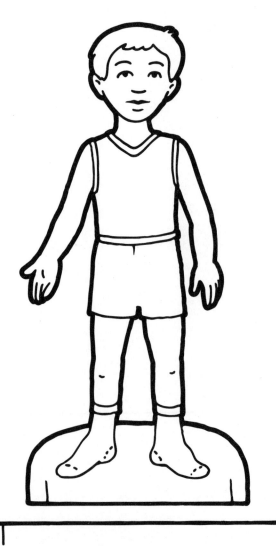

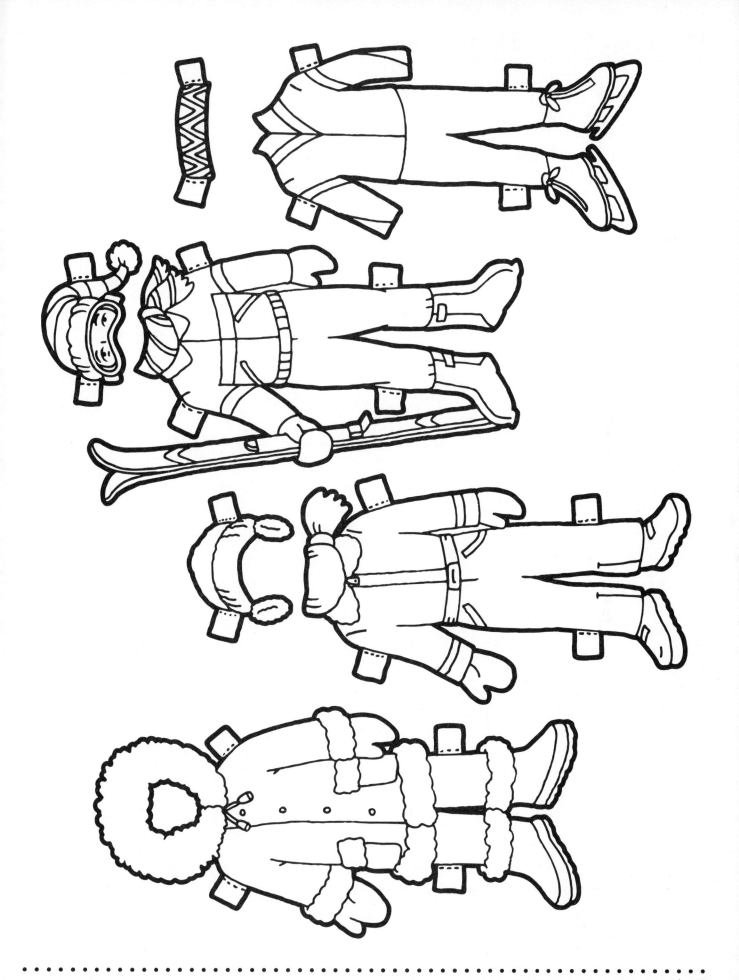

Polar Animals

Some animals live in places where it is cold all year long. Color all of the animals and the place they live. Then, cut out all of the animals and place them in the landscape. You can either move them around or paste them in one place.

My Winter Holidays

Write about how you celebrate your favorite winter holiday.

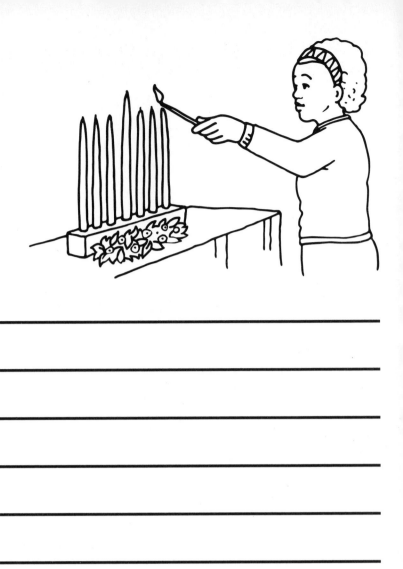

_____

_____

_____

_____

_____

_____

_____

Let's Celebrate Hanukkah!

Every year in December, Jewish people celebrate Hanukkah. For each night of Hanukkah, people light another candle on the menorah. The center candle stays lit the whole time. Color and decorate the menorah and candle flames, then cut them out. For each day of Hanukkah, add another flame to the menorah using glue.

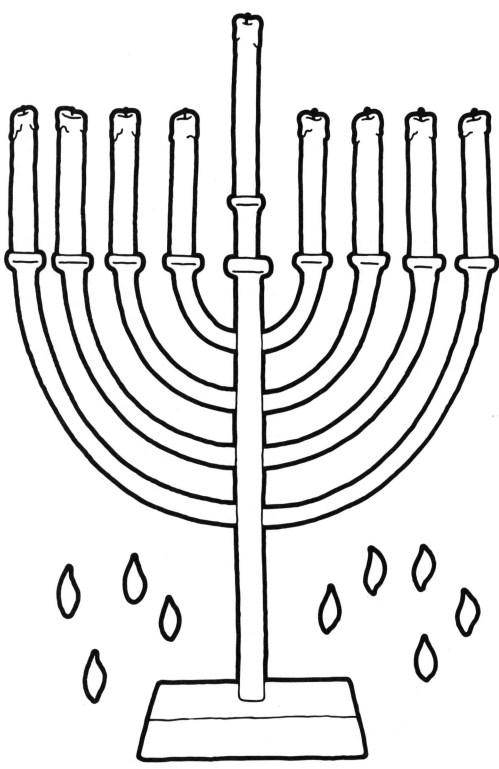

Spin the Dreidel

A dreidel is a special top that Jewish children play with during Hanukkah. Decorate and cut out the dreidel pattern. Use tape or glue to put the sides together. Attach a pencil, straw, or wooden craft stick through the top so you can spin your dreidel.

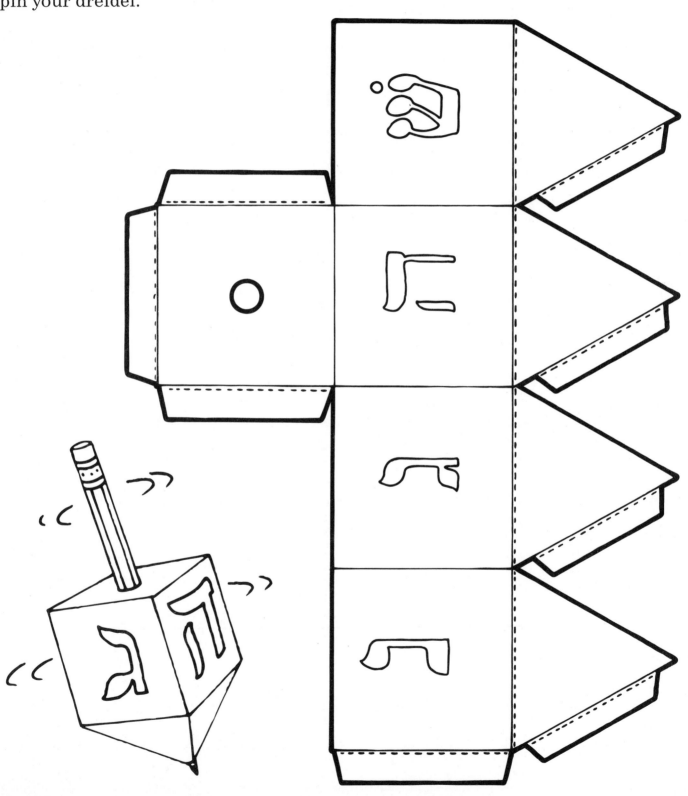

Poinsettia Day

December 12 is Poinsettia Day. Poinsettias are bright red flowers that many people like to put out during the holidays. Color and cut out the poinsettia blossoms. You can attach them to pencils, straws, or wooden sticks to make your own bouquet.

Wright Brothers Day

December 17 is Wright Brothers Day. The Wright Brothers were the first people to build and fly an airplane! Today, there are many different kinds of airplanes that people use every day. Color and cut out all of the airplanes, and attach them to a hanger with string to make your own mobile!

My Wish List!

Write down or draw what you hope to receive for the holidays!

'Tis the Season

Follow the garland around the tree to the top before the boy puts on the final touch—the star!

Answer on page 96.

A Holiday Card

Many people send each other cards for the holidays. Write a note or draw a picture in this card, and give it to someone special!

• • • **A Holiday Card** •

A Christmas Stocking

Here is a Christmas stocking just for you! You can color and decorate it with words or pictures that tell about Christmas or things that are special to you. When you're done, you can cut it out and hang it up at school or at home.

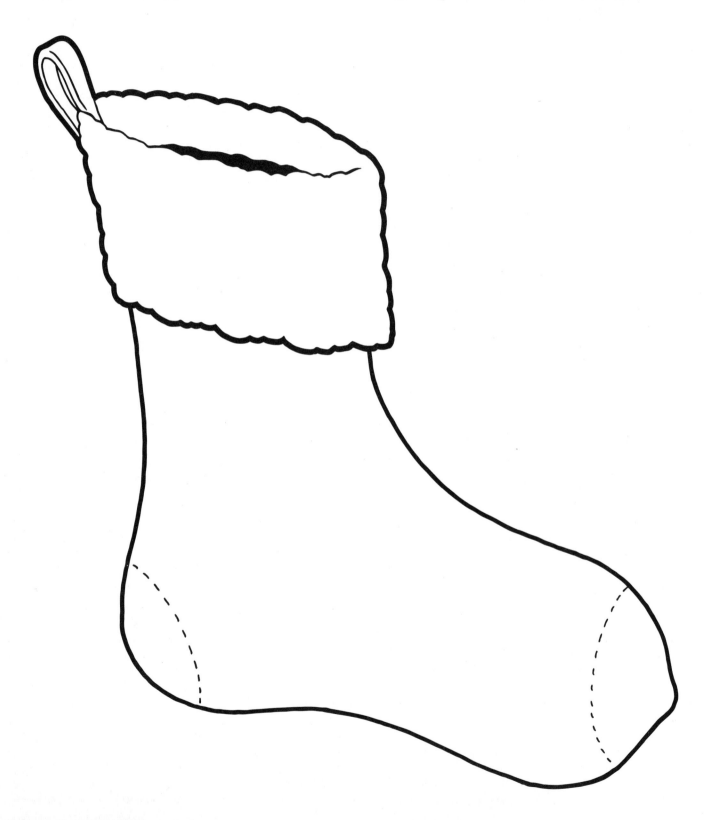

A Batch of Christmas Cookies

Christmas would not be complete without some cookies! Color and decorate these cookies with glue and glitter and then cut them out. Glue magnets to the back if you'd like to decorate your refrigerator. They will look good enough to eat!

An Elf Assembly Line

Santa's elves are working hard to make enough toys for Christmas, but they need help! In the blank space on the assembly line, draw some toys that you would like the elves to make! You can also color the elves.

Hang Up the Ornaments!

These ornaments aren't ready to go on the Christmas tree yet! Color and decorate them with your favorite Christmas designs. Then, you can cut them out and hang them in the classroom or on your Christmas tree at home!

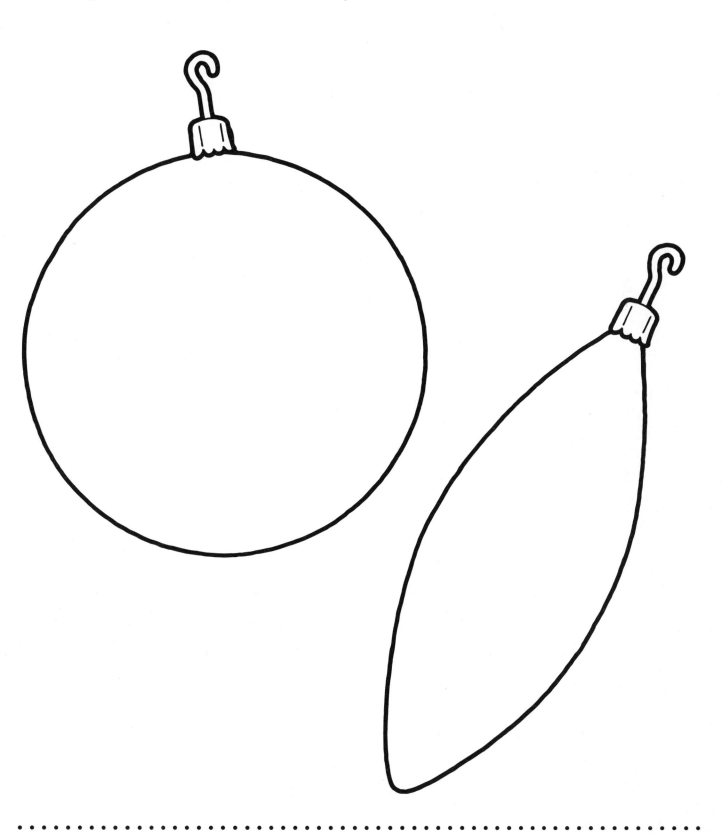

• • • • • **Hang Up the Ornaments!** • • • • • •

The Best Present!

What is the best Christmas present you have ever received? Draw a picture of your favorite present in the frame below. You can also draw a picture of something you have given to someone as a gift, too!

My Favorite Present

What Kwanzaa Means to Me

Write about how you celebrate Kwanzaa or something you learned about it.

_____

_____

_____

_____

_____

_____

_____

• • • **What Kwanzaa Means to Me** • • •

A Kwanzaa Harvest

Part of Kwanzaa is celebrating the harvest of fruits and vegetables. Color and cut out the fruits, vegetables, and basket. Put them all together for your own Kwanzaa harvest feast!

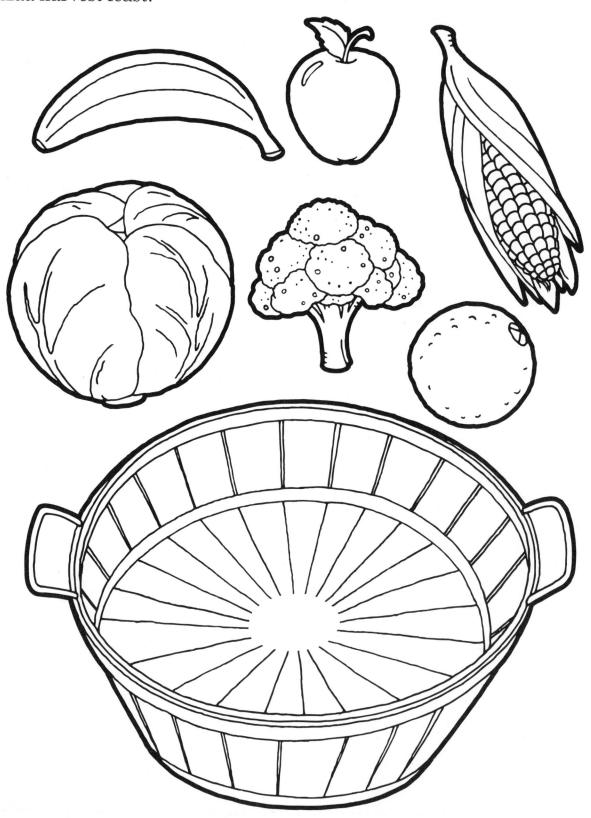

Put on Your Party Hat!

Get ready to celebrate the New Year with your very own party hat! Decorate and cut out the pieces of the hat and attach them so they fit around your head. Use an extra strip of blank paper if you need to make the hat bigger. Have an adult cut the center out of a paper plate to make a brim for your hat!

Happy New Year!

My New Year's Resolutions

What changes do you want to make for the new year?
Write about them!

_____

_____

_____

_____

_____

_____

_____

Winter Sports

Happy New Year!

A Birthday Crown

Celebrate this month's birthdays with this fun crown. Write your name on the crown, then color and cut it out. Tape or glue the ends together to finish your crown!

What Will Happen in the New Year?

What do you think will happen this year? Write about something you predict for the coming year.

_____

_____

_____

_____

_____

_____

_____

_____

What Not to Wear?

Circle the item of clothing that doesn't belong with the others in each group.

Answers on page 96.

Time of the Season

The weather in summer and winter can be very different! Try and think about all of the ways you can show what the two seasons are like. In the spaces below, you can draw and color how things look during the summer and during the winter.

Catching Snowflakes

Did you know that every snowflake has a different shape? Now you can add your own special snowflake to this winter scene. Design and draw it in the space below! You can make any shape you like, even something fun or silly!

Warm Winter Treats

Sometimes it is nice to eat or drink something hot on a cold day to keep toasty warm. Color all of the food and the table, and then serve it up. On the empty bowl, mug, and plate, draw some of this hot food or your favorites so that you can enjoy a winter feast!

College Football Tic-Tac-Toe

Lots of college football teams play championship bowl games on New Year's Day. Join in the fun with this football tic-tac-toe game! Color and cut out the helmets, and then challenge a friend to play tic-tac-toe on the grid using the helmets instead of writing X's and O's. Three of the same helmets in a row wins!

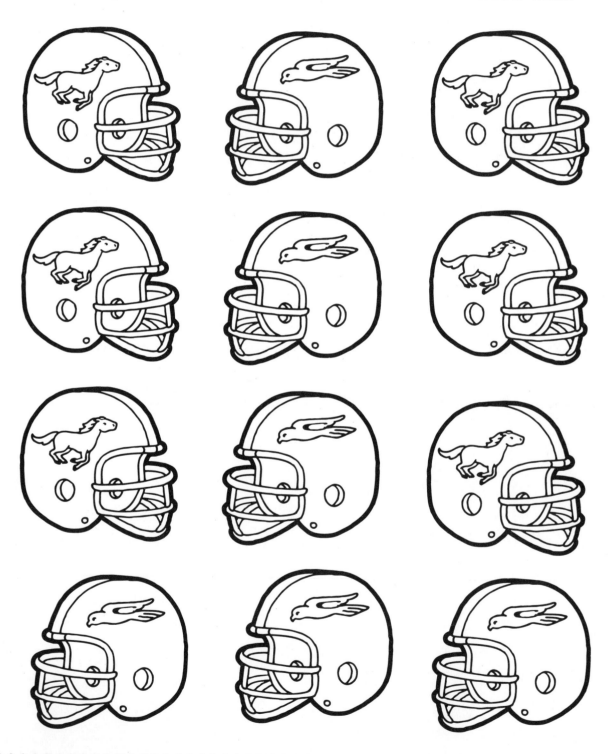

Write a Letter!

Did you know that Letter Writing Week is in January? Why not write a letter and send it to someone special? Using the stationery, write a letter or draw some pictures for someone you like. Cut out, fold, and tape or glue the envelope so you can put your letter inside. Then, you can give the letter to a special person! If you want to mail your letter, ask your parent or a grown-up for help.

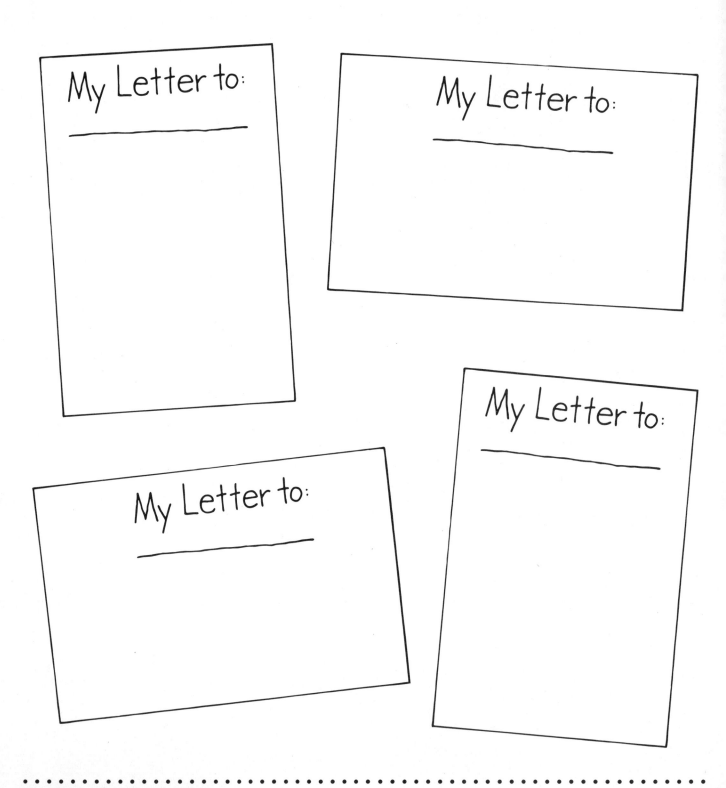

My Letter to:
_____

My Letter to:
_____

My Letter to:
_____

My Letter to:
_____

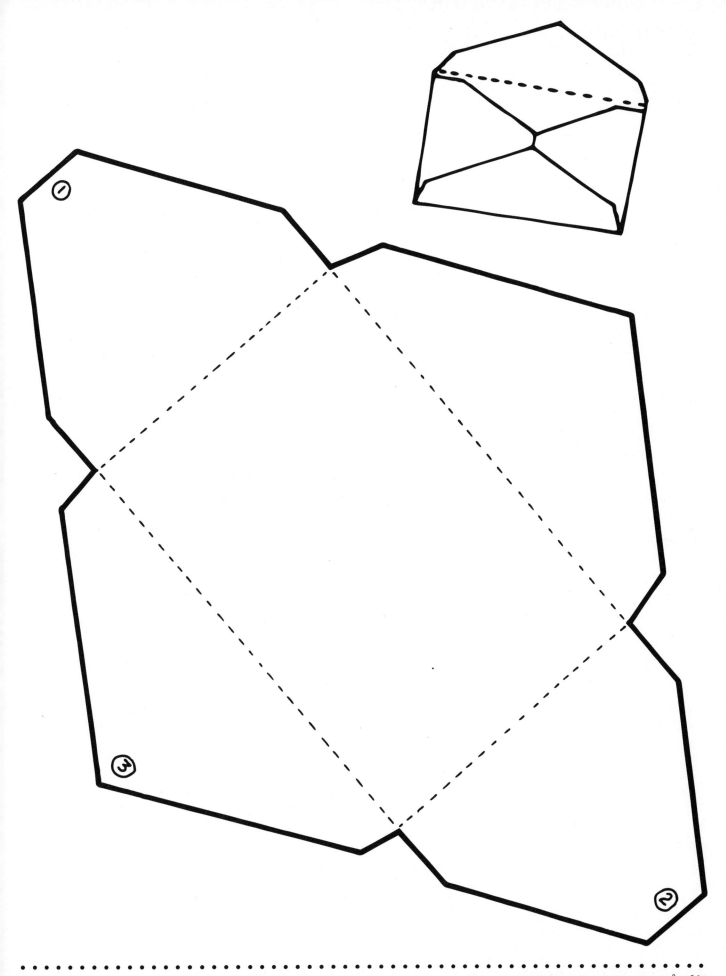

Hibernating Animals

In the winter, some animals go to sleep to save their energy. This is called hibernating. Color all of the animals and the animal den. Draw a line from the animals that hibernate to the den. Ask a grown-up if you need help!

What Does a Penguin Do?

Do you know what penguins do? On one side of the iceberg, draw and color a penguin doing something that you know penguins like to do. On the other side, draw and color a penguin doing something silly that penguins do not usually do!

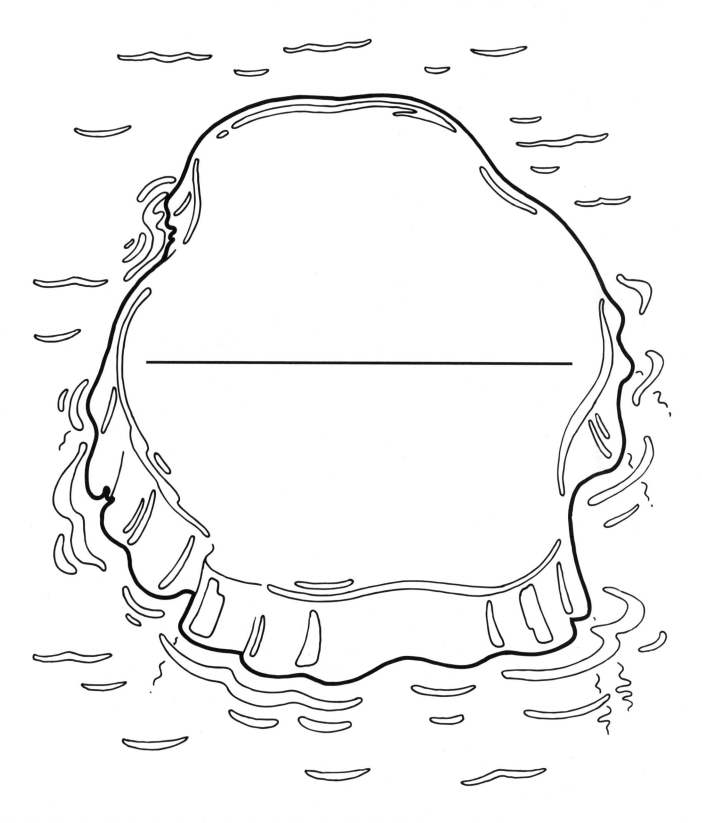

What's the Best Part of Winter?

What's your favorite part of the winter season? Write about what makes winter special to you!

_____

_____

_____

_____

_____

_____

_____

Mountains of Fun

Vincent loves having fun in the snowy winter. Can you figure out what he likes to do? Connect the dots from 1 through 101 to see Vincent up on his favorite mountain.

Answer on page 96.

Let's Play Hockey!

Hockey is a fun winter sport. Can you help this boy and girl get ready for their hockey game? Color and cut out the dolls and all of their hockey clothes. Then dress them up so they're ready to hit the ice!

Let's Play Hockey!

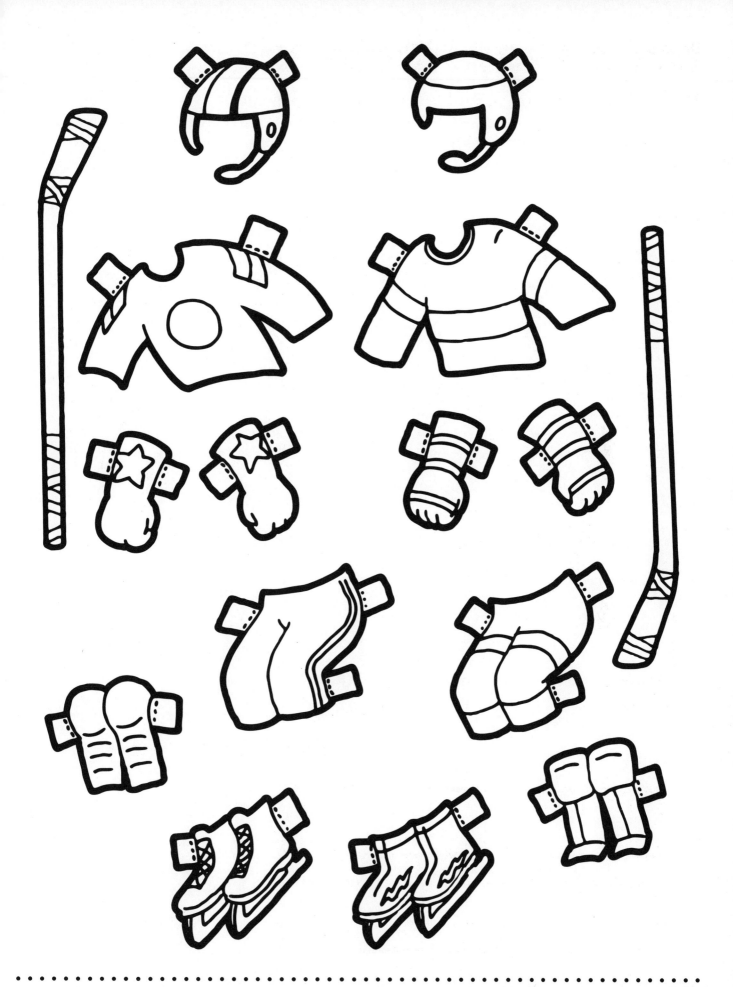

Bald Eagle Appreciation Day

Did you know that January 17 is Bald Eagle Appreciation Day? Color and cut out both sides of the bald eagle. Fold the two sides together and attach them with tape or glue. Attach a string and ask a grown-up to hang up your bald eagle so it can soar high above!

Bowling Blunders

Bowling is a fun thing to do when it's too cold to play outside. Can you find 12 or more errors in this bowling scene?

Answers on page 96.

Dr. Martin Luther King Jr. Day

January 18 is Dr. Martin Luther King Jr. Day. He worked hard so that all people could have the same rights. In his famous "I Have a Dream" speech, he said that he dreamed that one day all people could live together peacefully. Do you have a dream or idea about how the future could be better? Is there something you would change so everybody could be happier? Draw your dream in the dream bubble.

Dr. Martin Luther King Jr.

Write something you learned about Dr. Martin Luther King Jr.

_____

_____

_____

_____

_____

_____

A Chinese New Year Dragon!

Chinese New Year is a time of fun and celebration for Chinese people. Dancers in dragon costumes are part of the holiday. Color and cut out this dragon mask so you can celebrate, too! Ask a grown-up to help you attach some string so you can wear your mask.

Light the Lanterns!

Lanterns are an important decoration for the Chinese New Year. Color and cut out the lanterns and string them together to get ready for your own celebration!

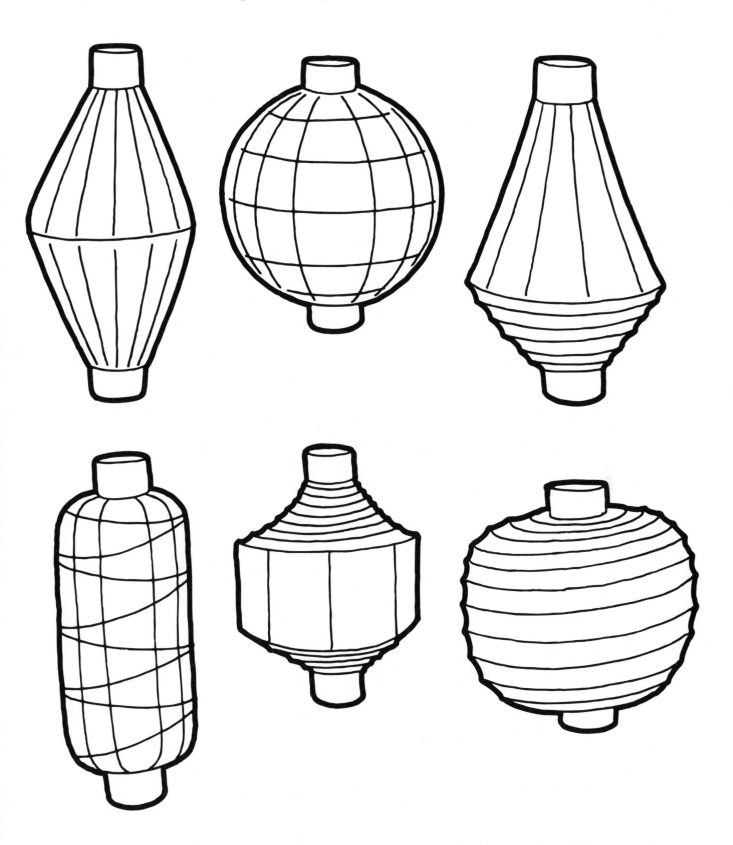

Make a Pie!

A warm slice of pie is a great winter treat. Help the baker make a pie! Color and cut out all of the pictures. Put them in the right order to show how the baker made the pie. You can tape or glue the pictures to a piece of paper, if you like.

Secret Spaces

These eight objects are hidden somewhere in the picture. Can you find and circle them all?

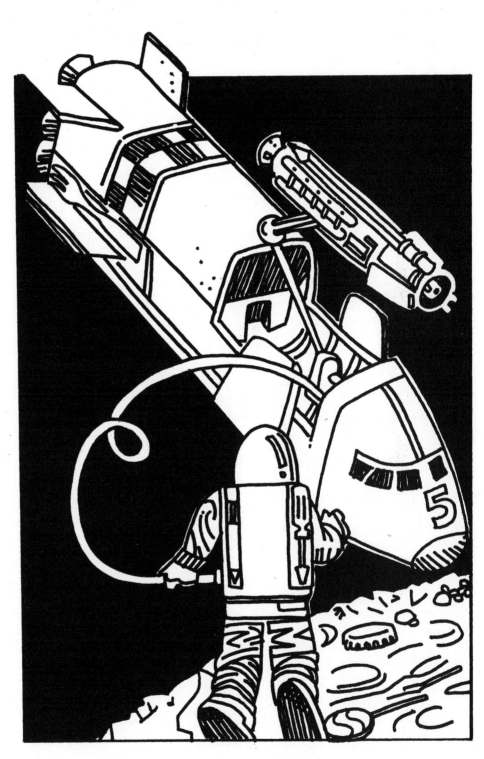

Answers on page 96.

Where Do We Live?

Some animals live in places that are always hot and some live in places that are always cold. Color all of the animals, and put a circle around the ones that live in cold places. Can you find them all?

Share a Hug!

January 23 is National Hugging Day! In the picture frame, draw somebody special you like to hug!

Presidents' Day

Valentine's Day

Tell 'Em It's Your Birthday!

Celebrate your February birthday with this fun birthday megaphone. Color and cut out the megaphone, and use tape or glue to make it into a cone. Use it to let everyone know it's your birthday!

It's Groundhog Day!

February 2 is Groundhog Day! When the groundhog pops out of his hole on this day, if he sees his shadow, it means winter will last six more weeks. If he doesn't, it means winter is almost over! Color and cut out the groundhog and his hole. Then you can make him pop out of his hole and make your own weather predictions!

The Groundhog's Prediction

Make a fun drawing to celebrate Groundhog Day! In the frame you can either draw a picture of the groundhog or of you and your friends enjoying the weather that the groundhog predicted.

Remember to Brush!

February is Children's Dental Health Month. Part of good dental health is making sure to brush your teeth at least twice every day! You can use this chart to keep track of when you brush during the week. Every time you brush in the morning and at night, mark the square for that day. You can color the spaces or use stickers, if you have them!

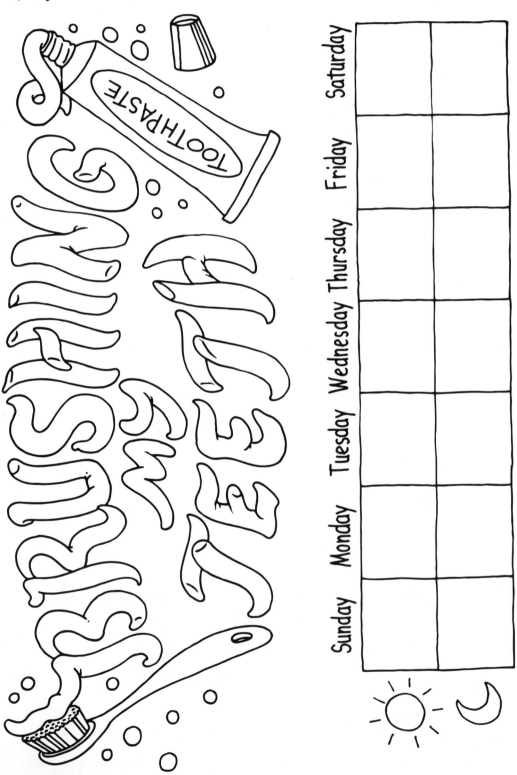

Choose Wisely!

Some things are good for your teeth and some things are not. Color all the items, and then put an X through the ones that are bad for teeth. (Hint: Things with lots of sugar are bad for teeth!)

Answers on page 96.

The Super Bowl

The Super Bowl is a championship football game that lots of people like to watch on TV! Celebrate this fun game by decorating the helmet. You can make it look like the helmet from your favorite team or you can create a brand-new helmet!

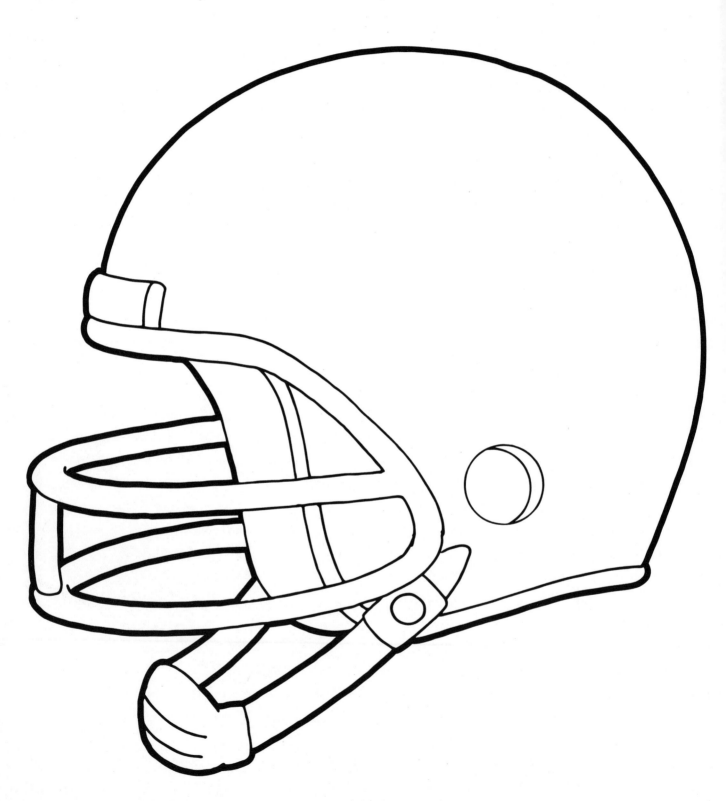

National Pancake Week

Did you know that National Pancake Week is in February? Color and cut out the skillet and spatula. Use scrap paper to make fun pancakes in any shape you want. Then, give them a flip in the pan to cook them up!

Winter Sports

Even though it's cold outside, there are lots of fun sports you can play in the winter! Color and cut out all of the winter sports equipment, and paste them to a piece of paper to make your own winter sports poster! You can also add other images or words you would like to see.

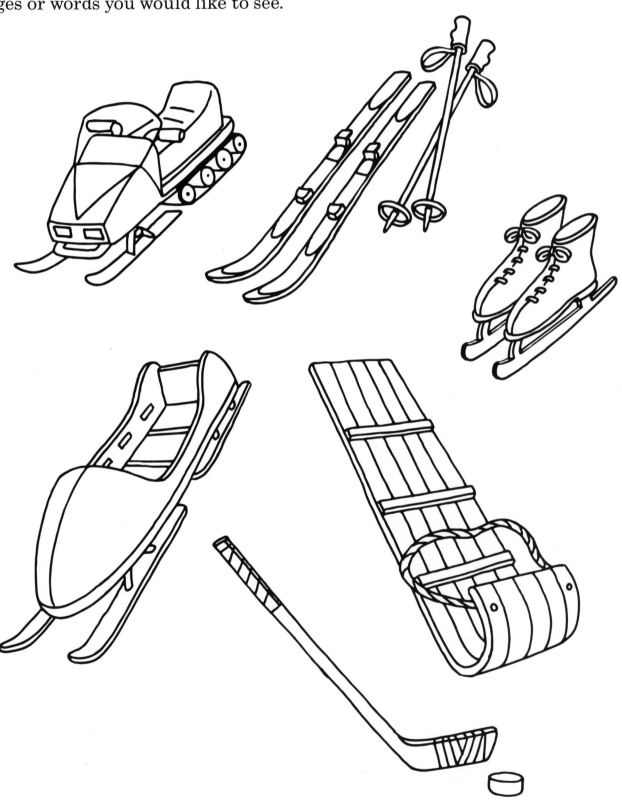

Ski Jumping

One exciting winter sporting event is the ski jump. You can draw one skier (or lots of skiers) using the ramp to do fantastic jumps!

What a Bubble!

Did you know that February 5 is Bubblegum Day? Something seems out of order in the pictures below. Color the pictures and number them to show the correct order. You can also cut them out and put them in order, if you like!

Celebrate Black History Month

February is Black History Month. It's a time when everyone can learn about African American history and culture. Kente cloth is a special kind of woven fabric that people have made in Africa for a long time. Today, it is a special symbol for people with African heritage. Use lots of bright colors to decorate these kente cloth bookmarks to celebrate Black History Month!

It's Abraham Lincoln's Birthday!

Did you know that February 12 is Abraham Lincoln's birthday? He was known for wearing a tall hat called a stovepipe hat. Cut out and put together the stovepipe hat so you can look just like Lincoln!

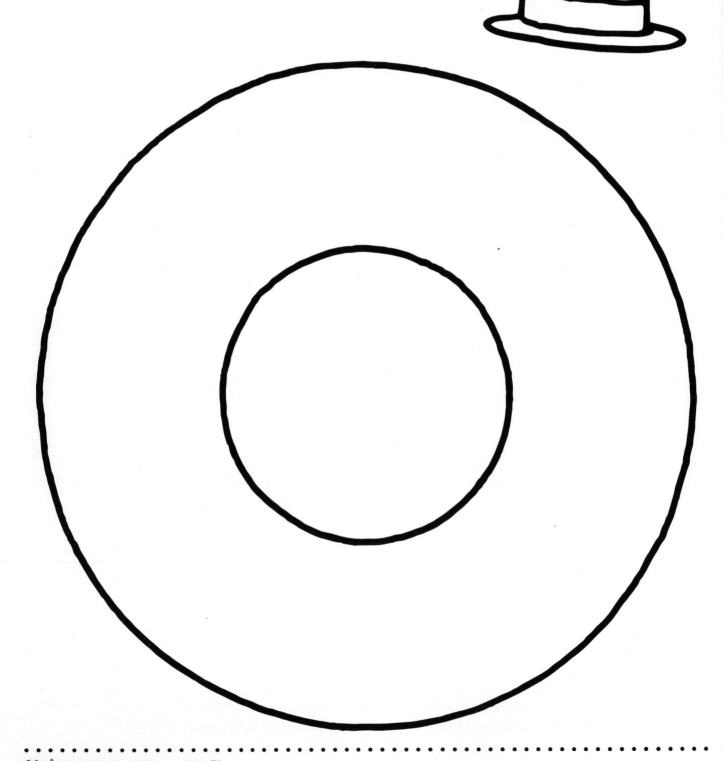

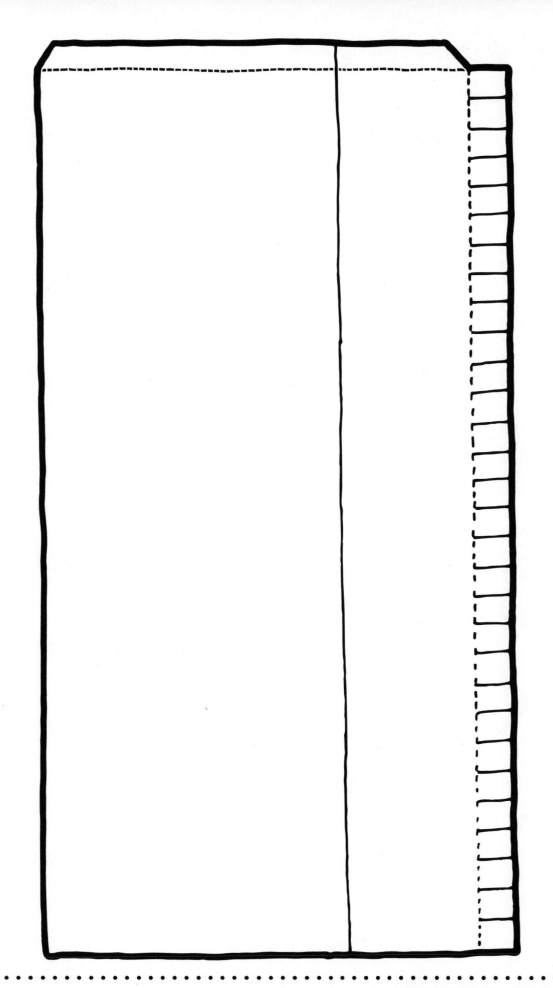

Log Cabin Lincoln

When Abraham Lincoln was president, he lived in the White House. When he was young, he lived in a log cabin. Color and cut out the logs and the cabin pendant. Tape or glue the logs into rings, attaching them to one another to make a paper chain. Attach the rings to the log cabin to make a log cabin necklace! You can paste a penny on the cabin to show that it's Lincoln's house!

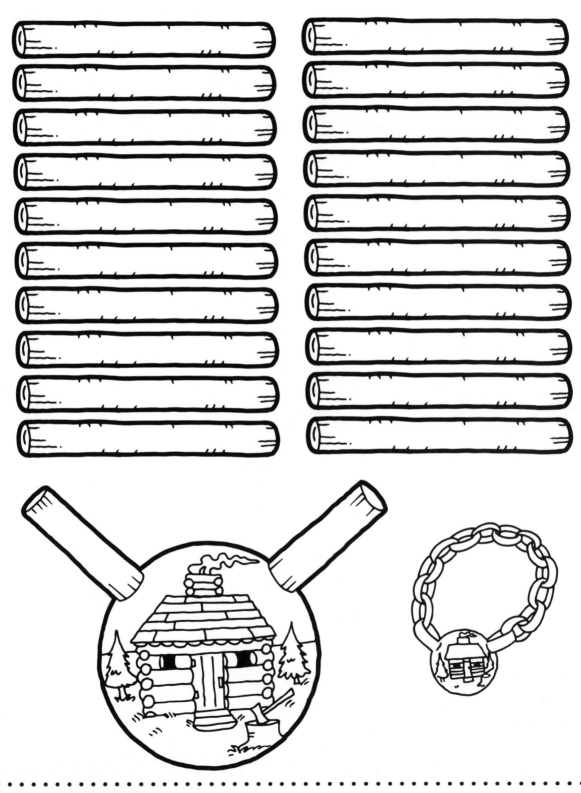

Will You Be Mine?

How many words can you make from the word *Valentine?* Can you find 20?

_____   _____   _____   _____

_____   _____   _____   _____

_____   _____   _____   _____

_____   _____   _____   _____

Answers on page 96.

A Special Valentine

Valentine's Day is a fun time to give cards to your friends and family! Color and decorate this Valentine, and give it to somebody special!

Special Delivery!

It's time to deliver Valentines! But where should you put them? Make a Valentine's Day mailbox so your friends have a place to deliver Valentines to you. Decorate the mailbox with your name and fun Valentine's Day drawings or designs. Paste it to an empty paper bag or box to make your own mailbox!

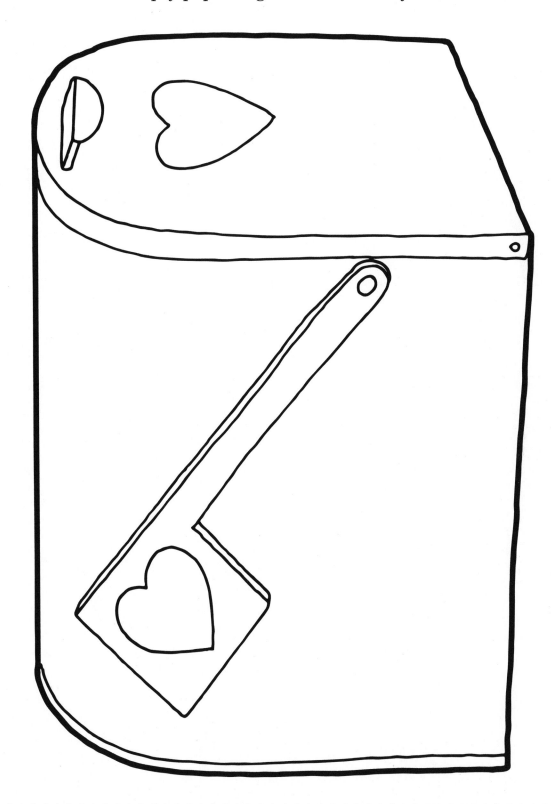

Which Valentine Is Mine?

Help! These kids can't find their Valentines! Look at the kids and at the cards to see which ones match. Draw a line from each kid to his or her Valentine. Each kid will have only one.

Hearts and Cupids

Decorate your home or classroom to get in the Valentine's Day spirit! Color and cut out the hearts and cupids. Attach them to a piece of yarn or ribbon to make a fun Valentine's Day garland!

Heartbreaker Challenge

Connect the nine hearts by drawing only four lines—without lifting your pencil!

Answer on page 96.

A Scouting Challenge

This Boy Scout and Girl Scout need your help! The Boy Scout wants to go canoeing. Can you draw a line from him to everything he needs? The Girl Scout wants to go camping. Can you draw a line from her to everything she needs?

Answers on page 96.

Take a Spin on a Ferris Wheel!

Did you know that February 14 is also Ferris Wheel Day? Color the pieces of the Ferris wheel and the scene on the next page. Cut out the wheel, and attach it to the base with a metal fastener so your Ferris wheel can spin!

I Cannot Tell a Lie

Have you heard the story about George Washington and the cherry tree? If you haven't, ask an adult to tell it to you! To celebrate Washington's Birthday on February 22, color the cherry tree. Put a quarter behind the paper and use a red crayon to make rubbings of quarters to put cherries on the tree. If you don't have a quarter, you can draw the cherries.

Washington's White Wig

George Washington is famous for wearing a powdered wig, but it looks like he's missing his wig! Can you paste cotton balls on the picture to make Washington a new wig? If you don't have cotton balls, you can draw a new wig.

Mardi Gras Mask

Mardi Gras is a time for fun and celebration! Lots of people like to wear colorful masks to celebrate. Color and decorate the Mardi Gras mask. Use tape or glue to attach the fun decorations.

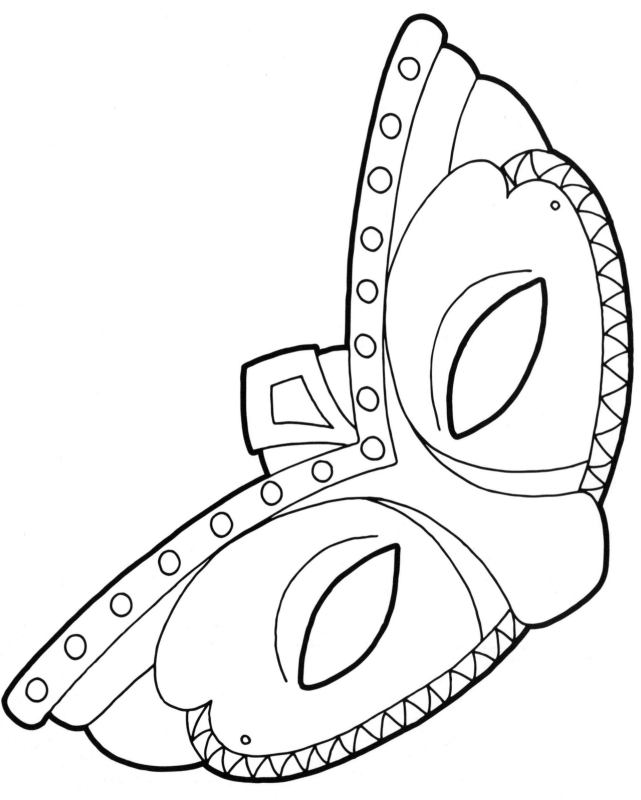

Answers

'Tis the Season
(page 26)

What Not to Wear? *(page 42)*
sandals, dress

Mountains of Fun
(page 53)

Bowling Blunders
(page 57)
boy on skateboard, missing lane 4, turtle as bowling ball, soldier as pin, hoop on lane, three bowling balls on one lane, girl bowling wrong way, upside down bowling pin, skeeball target in place of pins, barefoot boy, oversize shoe, duck and water

in alley, upside down glasses, beachball, "Pineheads"

Secret Spaces
(page 63)

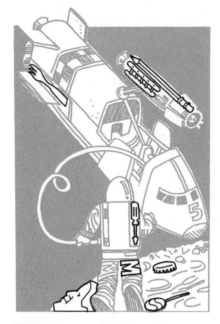

Choose Wisely!
(page 73)

Will You Be Mine?
(page 83)
ail, ale, alien, alive, ant, anvil, ate, eat, eaten, eel, enliven, entail,

eve, even, event, evil, inane, inlet, inn, innate, invent, lane, late, lean, leave, lei, lenient, lent, let, lie, lien, line, linen, lint, lit, live, liven, nail, naïve, native, navel, neat, neaten, net, nil, nine, tail, tale, tan, tea, teal, tee, ten, tie, tile, tin, tine, vain, valet, van, vat, veal, veil, vein, vent, vet, via, vial, vie, vile, vine, vital

Heartbreaker Challenge
(page 88)

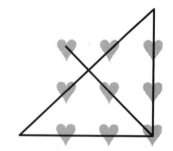

A Scouting Challenge *(page 89)*

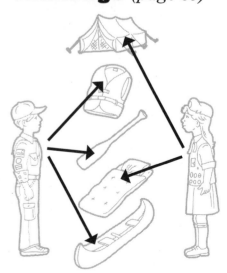

TEACHERS' FAVORITES™

Fun Activities for

SPRING!

Reproducible Patterns for Paper Crafts, Coloring Pages, Decorations, and More!

Illustrations by Rick Ewigleben

Publications International, Ltd.

Contents

Spring into Action!

It's easy enough to color an Easter bunny or cut out a kite. But having inventive and engaging activities that students respond to, have fun with, and maybe even learn from can be a daunting task. This is true whether you lead a classroom, Sunday school class, scout troop, or a home filled with eager learners. The adaptable projects featured in *Teachers' Favorites*™: *Fun Activities for Spring!* will help you challenge your students with educational activities and purely fun seasonal projects.

Each season in this four-book series offers up a unique buffet of holidays, milestones, sports, and activities. Spring is the time for Easter, Mother's Day, birds, flowers, baseball, and kite flying. Students will enjoy relevant crafts that can be hung, worn, read, laminated, given as gifts, or used to decorate the room or bulletin board.

This book includes the following types of activities:

• Coloring
• Writing
• Math
• Paper crafts
• Games, such as look-and-find, connect the dots, and mazes

For craft projects, take the time to go over the instructions carefully. Also, make sure you have all the materials on hand before you get started. Here are just a few of the materials that are required for most projects:

Paper: Since the projects in this book will need to be photocopied for each student, be sure to have plenty of paper. Most projects can be copied on regular copy paper, but some projects (such as paper dolls and cutouts that stand) should be copied on heavier stock or construction paper. If you do not have access to heavier stock or your copier cannot accommodate construction paper, you can glue the project's paper to construction paper to make it sturdier. For some projects, such as the card for Mother's Day, it is important that you don't see through the paper. In such cases, you might want to glue construction paper to the back of the paper.

Glue and tape: Some projects call for glue and/or clear tape. If you use glue, make sure it is water-base and nontoxic.

Scissors: Many projects call for cutting out pieces. Some require cutting slits or poking holes. For younger children, you may need to do the cutting yourself—or have older children help. Always have safety scissors on hand for smaller hands!

Brads: Some projects call for brass brads to hold pieces together. If you do not have those on hand, you can substitute with twist ties.

Art supplies: Children can use crayons, markers, or paint to color these projects. If children will be painting, be aware that acrylic paint will dry permanently, though when wet it is easily cleaned up with water. Make sure children clean painting tools thoroughly when they are finished painting.

Art smock: Make sure children wear smocks or old shirts to protect clothes while working with paints and other messy materials.

Some children will be able to complete the crafts with little help, but at times your assistance will be needed. Other projects just need a watchful eye. So it is best that you review the project ahead of time and then make a decision about your role.

Flex Time
Another great thing about the crafts, coloring pages, and writing pages in this book is that they provide for versatility— which definitely comes in handy when working with children of

differing skill levels. The crafts can be simplified or made more complex depending on need.

Coloring pages are simple enough for younger children, but older children may want to challenge themselves by adding patterns, textures, or even decorations. Likewise, the writing pages are great for older children to let their imaginations flow in creating original stories, while beginning writers may use them to copy a few words or dictate longer stories to an adult. If your group is of mixed ages, consider taking a teamwork approach that combines the imaginative approach of a younger child and the writing skills of an older child.

Great Clips

Clip art pages are great for all kinds of applications. You can use a copy machine to increase the size of the seasonal images to make them suitable for wall or bulletin board decorations. Likewise, you can use the copier to make images smaller for use on worksheets, bulletins, notes to parents, or any other application you can dream up. Incorporate the clip art images to create seasonal birthday cards or stationery, or use them to add a decorative element to any other project.

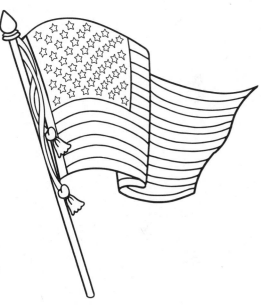

In the Mix

All of the projects presented in this book, from the simplest to the most elaborate, are just ideas to get you started. Feel free to alter the designs by choosing different materials or embellishing in any number of unique ways. Give your imagination free rein as you play around with materials and these base ideas. Encourage students to come up with their own unique variations on these themes, and keep them in mind for later uses. You can jump off in any direction, keeping these projects as fun and fresh as the first time you tried them. When it comes to creating fun springtime activities, the sky is the limit!

Spring Is Here!

March Holidays

The Robin's Nest

After spending the winter down south, many species of birds head back
north when the weather warms. In the spring, birds build nests and
lay eggs. Have fun coloring this scene of a robin and her chicks!

Flying Birds

Cheer up the classroom with colorful, flying birds! Color and cut out each pattern. Cut slits and punch holes where indicated, and then insert the wings. Connect the birds to the branch with string and watch them fly!

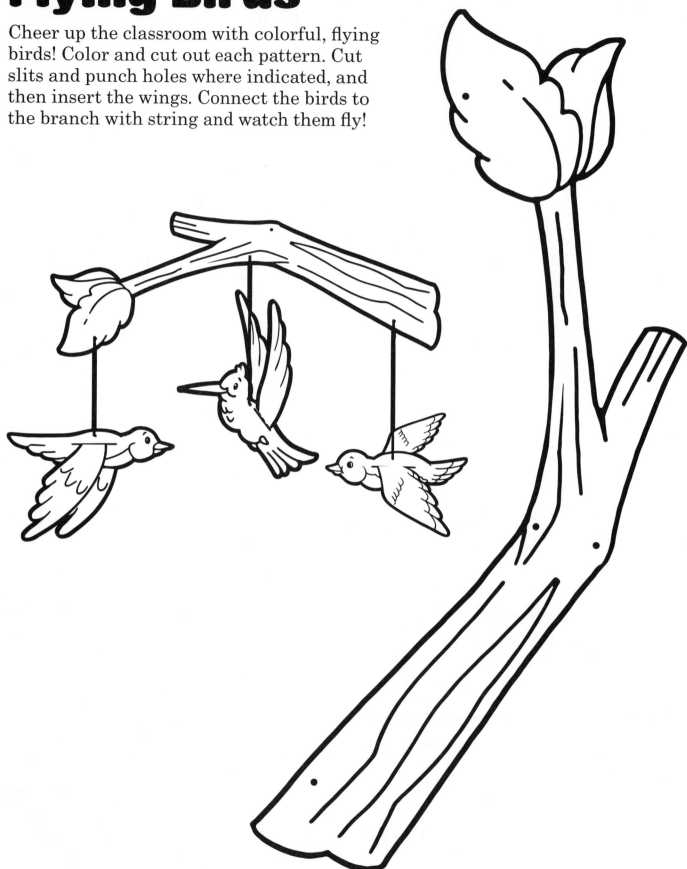

Bee-lieve It!

There's a lot of work to be done! Help this confused honeybee find her way out of the beehive so she can gather nectar with the rest of her crew.

Answer on page 96.

What's Your Middle Name?

Middle Name Pride Day is celebrated on the Friday of the first full
week in March. Write your first, middle, and last names on the nametag.
Write your middle name big so that everybody can see it. (If you do
not have a middle name, choose one that you would like to have!)

Hello, My Name Is...

———————————————

———————————————

———————————————

My Favorite Breakfast

National School Breakfast Week is celebrated every March to make kids aware of the importance of a good breakfast. Which of these foods do you like for breakfast? Color your favorites, cut them out, and place them on your dish and placemat. Enjoy your hearty meal!

March Madness

March is time for playoff basketball. Add up all the sums in the basketballs. Then put that total number in the home team's part of the scoreboard. Let's hope the home team wins!

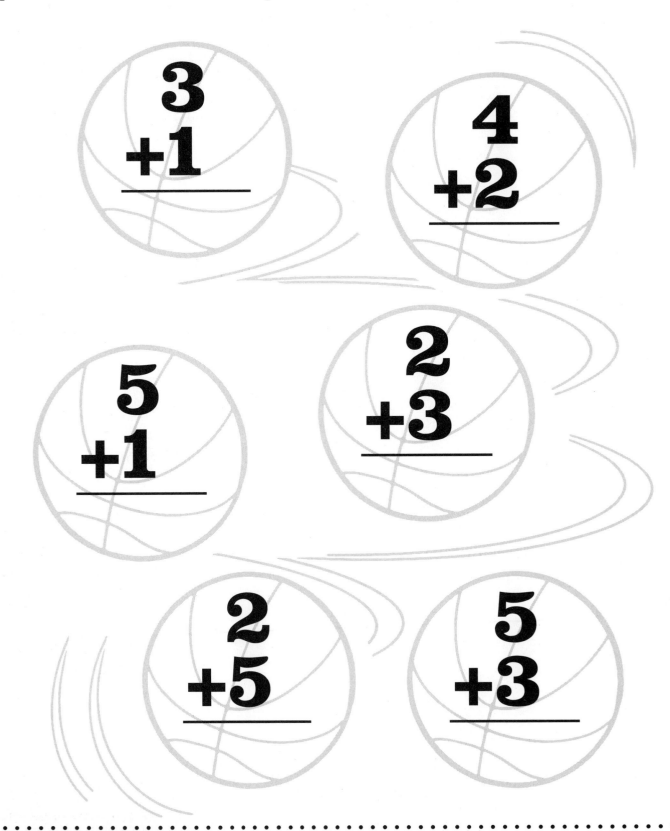

$$\begin{array}{r} 3 \\ +1 \\ \hline \end{array}$$

$$\begin{array}{r} 4 \\ +2 \\ \hline \end{array}$$

$$\begin{array}{r} 5 \\ +1 \\ \hline \end{array}$$

$$\begin{array}{r} 2 \\ +3 \\ \hline \end{array}$$

$$\begin{array}{r} 2 \\ +5 \\ \hline \end{array}$$

$$\begin{array}{r} 5 \\ +3 \\ \hline \end{array}$$

Answer on page 96.

Outside Fun

Things I Like to Do Outside

_____

_____

_____

_____

_____

_____

_____

_____

Slow Movin'

Help this snail along by connecting dots 1 through 13. Color the finished picture.

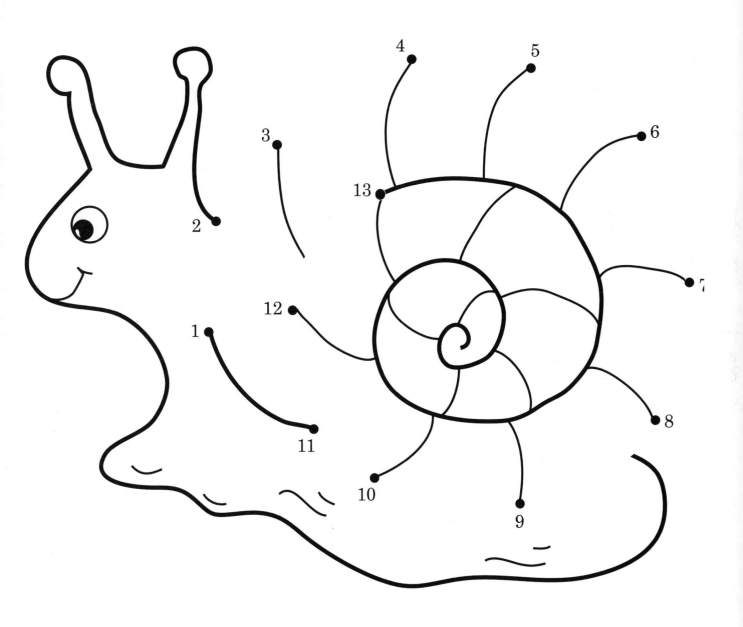

Answer on page 96.

Johnny Appleseed

March 11 is Johnny Appleseed Day. Color this scene while learning the tale of the man who helped plant apple trees across much of America.

A Is for Apple

Write down other words that begin with the letter A.

St. Patrick's Day

St. Patrick's Day is held on March 17. Pull out your crayons and make this leprechaun's dream come to life!

Best Wishes

According to tradition, if you find a four-leaf clover, you make a wish. What do you wish for?

I Wish For...

_____

_____

_____

_____

_____

_____

_____

_____

You, the Artist!

March is National Youth Art Month. Use this
blank canvas to express your creativity!

Home Fixes

Can you find 10 or more errors in this scene?

Answer on page 96.

Dancing Leprechaun

Make a leprechaun dance! Color and cut out the head, torso, and four limbs. Then use fasteners to put the leprechaun together. Sing a song and watch him dance!

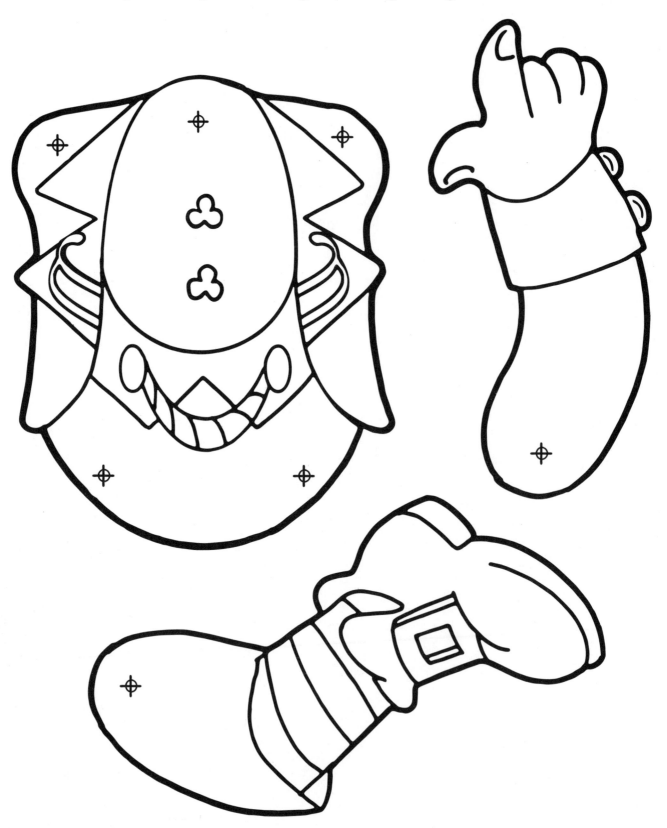

Pot of Treasure

While the leprechaun searches for a pot of gold, we found a pot of treasure just for you! Can you add the numbers on these coins to determine how much money you have?

Answer on page 96.

Flower Power

Help this flower grow by connecting dots 1 through 33. Color the finished picture.

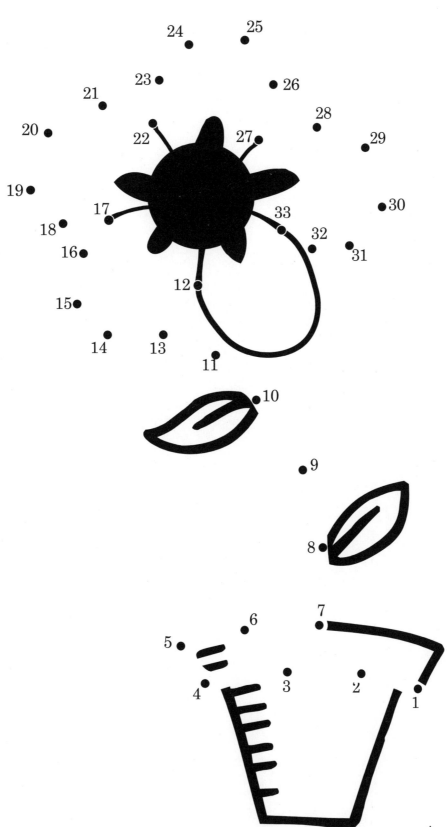

Answer on page 96.

In Like a Lion...

According to an old saying, March "comes in like a lion and goes out like a lamb." Discuss what that saying means. Then color, cut out, and fold these patterns to create a standup lion and lamb.

...Out Like a Lamb

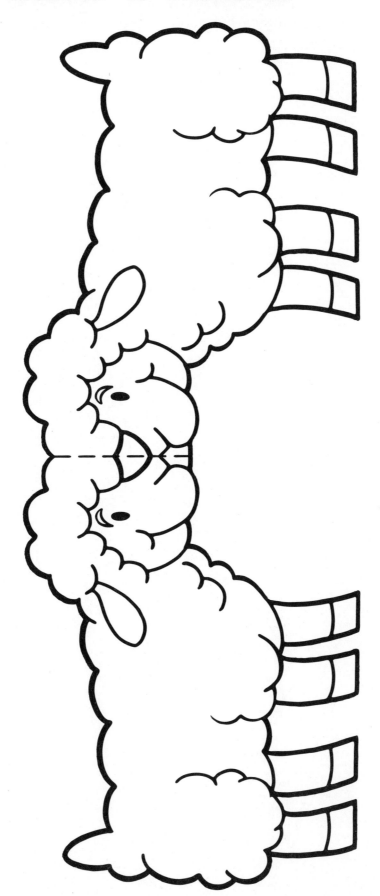

A Birthday Hat

Celebrate this month's birthdays with this festive hat.* Color, cut out, and fasten the hat. Then use a piece of string to secure the hat around your chin.

* Teacher: Enlarge this page at 150 percent to make the hats big enough for the children.

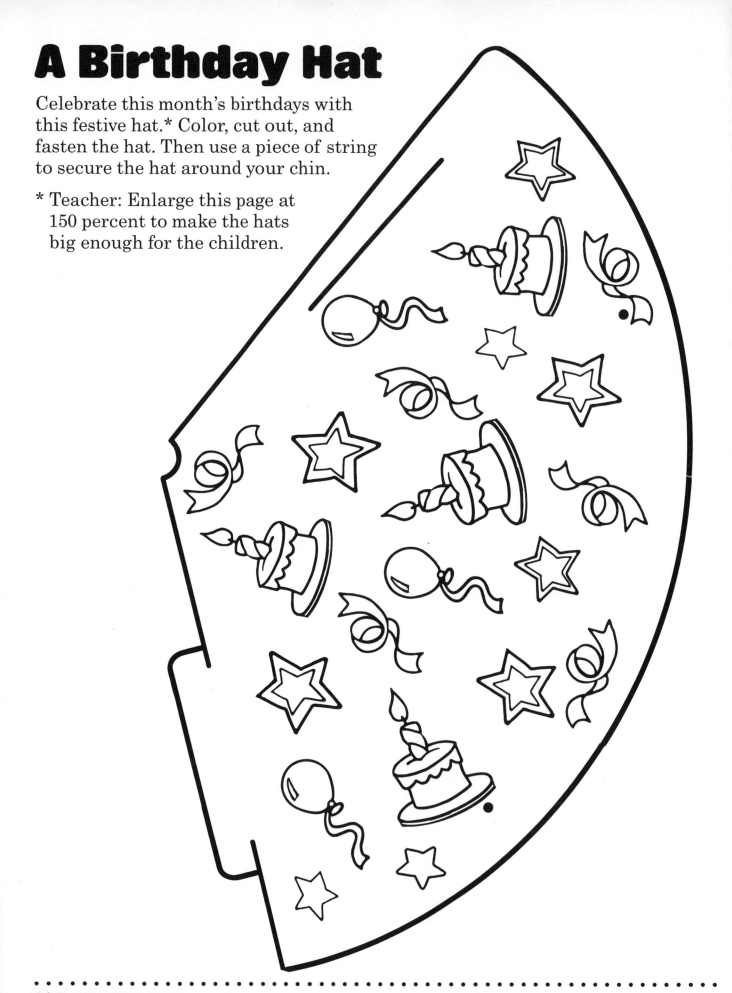

All-About-Me Quilt

March 21 is National Quilting Day. Fill out and color this all-about-me paper quilt.

Springtime Crossword

Look at the pictures on this page, and name each one. Then write the word in the correct numbered spaces.

Across

1.

3.

5.

6.

Down

1.

2.

4.

Answers on page 96.

Make a Splash!

Happy Easter!

April Showers Bring May Flowers

The rain that falls in April helps our flowers grow. Color and cut out the clouds, tulips, and daffodils. Punch holes where indicated. Use thread or string to attach the clouds and flowers to a hanger. It's the perfect "rainy day" activity!

Funny Face

Celebrate April Fool's Day (April 1) by making funny faces.
Color and cut out the hair, glasses, mouths, mustache, and beard.
Try different combinations to make all kinds of funny faces.

Laugh Out Loud!

On these lines, write some funny jokes. They can be jokes you have heard or those you make up yourself.

LOL Jokes

1. _____

_____

_____

2. _____

_____

_____

3. _____

_____

_____

It's Raining, It's Pouring

Look at the pictures on this page, and name each one. Write the word in the correct numbered spaces. Be sure to check to see if the word should be written across or down.

Across

3.

6.

Down

1.

2.

4.

5.

Answers on page 96.

Prepare the Firefighter

Can you dress these firefighters to get them ready for their next mission? Color and cut out the firefighters and their clothes/accessories. Fold the tabs to secure the clothes on the figures' bodies. The accessories can be glued or taped. Now they are ready for action!

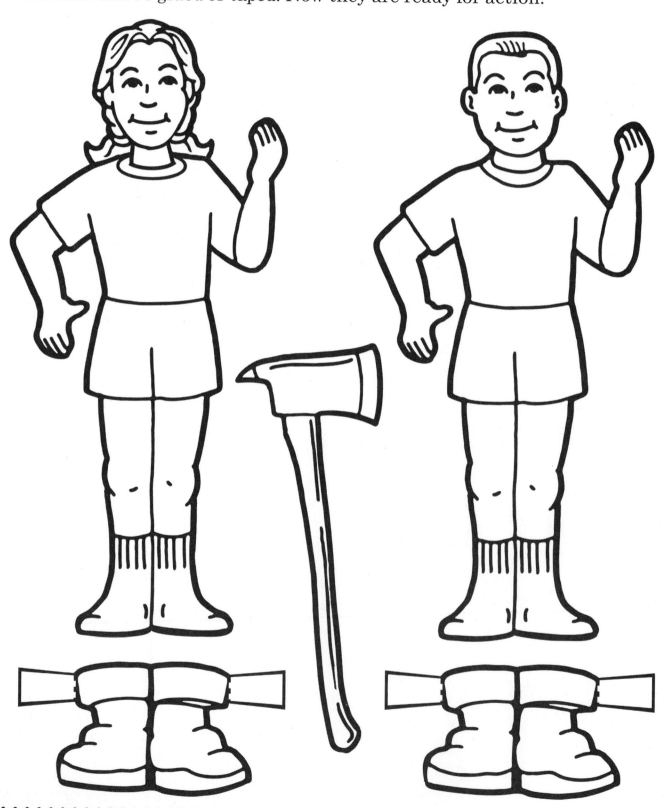

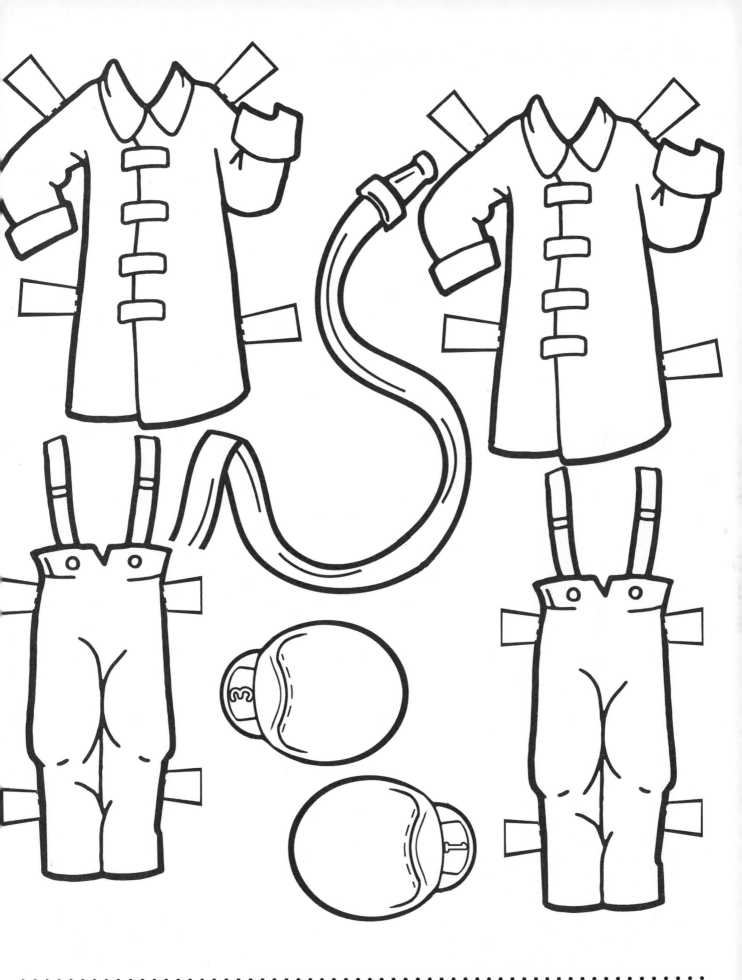

Rainy Day Fun

Things I Can Do on a Rainy Day

1. _____

_____

2. _____

_____

3. _____

_____

4. _____

_____

Cut out the entire picture below. After coloring the items, paste the whole picture on the side of a box. You will then have a "Rainy Day Box." Fill it with toys and other fun things that you can play with on a rainy day.

Standup Easter Eggs

It's time to design Easter eggs! Color the eggs and then cut them out.
Examine the diagram to learn how to create your own standup Easter eggs.

Easter Basket

Color this Easter basket and cut it out. It will make a festive holiday decoration for your classroom or home.

Easter Egg Glasses

It's time to get a little silly! Color and cut out these Easter egg glasses and put the pieces together. You'll need to tape the "hinges" so that the glasses will be secure enough to wear.

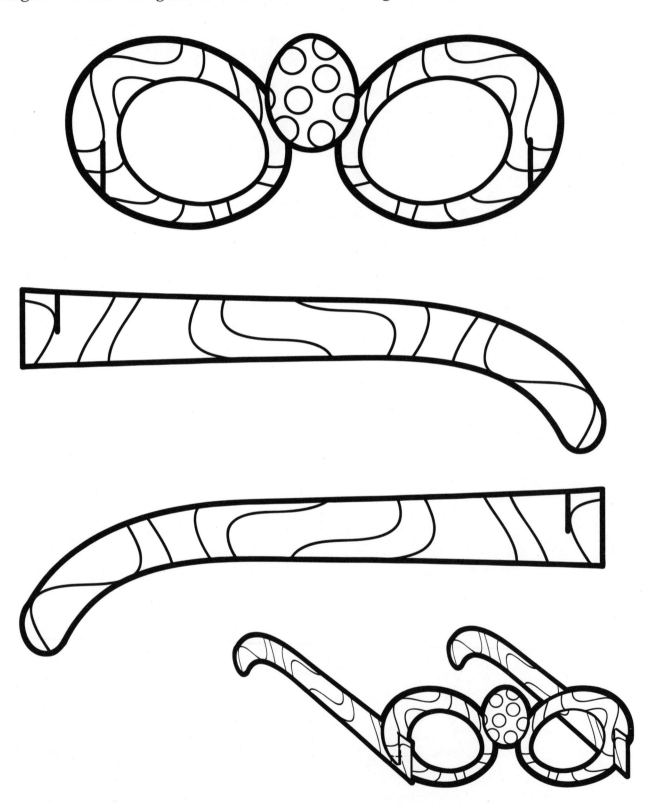

Standup Easter Bunny

Color, cut out, and fold this pattern to create your own standup Easter bunny.

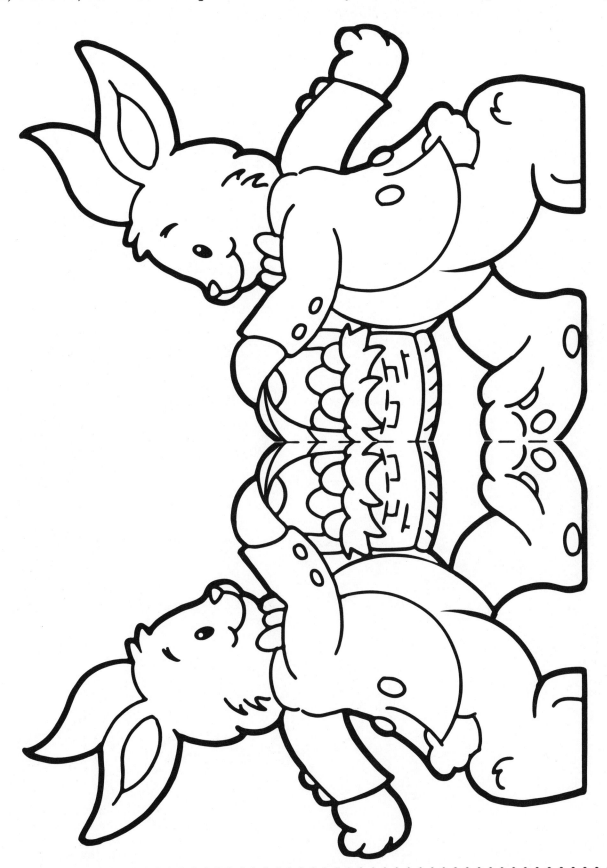

Easter Egg Hunt

Hidden in this picture is a bunch of Easter eggs. Try to find as many as you can. Finding 20 or more would be *egg*-citing!

Answer on page 96.

Count and Color Jellybeans

April 22 is National Jellybean Day. Color all the jellybeans in the jar with six different crayons: red, blue, purple, green, yellow, and orange. How many red jellybeans are there? Write that number next to the word *Red*. Do the same for the other colors. Add the six numbers. How many total jellybeans are in the jar?

Red _____

Blue _____

Purple _____

Green _____

Yellow _____

Orange _____

Total _____

Answer on page 96.

What's in *Your* Garden?

April is National Garden Month. Color and cut out all of the vegetables and fruits, then place them in the garden. Which ones are your favorites?

Teacher: This is the top of the picture.

America the Beautiful

April is Keep America Beautiful Month.
Have fun coloring this beautiful park scene.

Birthday Badge

Color and cut out this birthday badge. Don't forget to write your age on the middle line. Attach to your shirt with a piece of rolled-up tape.

I Am

Years Old

Fly a Kite

April is National Kite Month. On a windy day, go outside and fly one. In the meantime, cut out and color this mini kite. Add ribbon for a tail.

Kick It!

It's April, and that means it's time for spring soccer season. Color this kickin' scene. Later today, maybe you could play the game for real!

Celebrate Earth Day

April 22 is Earth Day. On this day, we learn how to take care of our environment and conserve Earth's resources.

On the globe below, color in the continents and oceans.

On the right-hand page, color the household objects. Then cut out the objects and the words. At home, you can tape them in appropriate places as reminders to save energy.

Lamp

Turn off the light when you are not in the room.

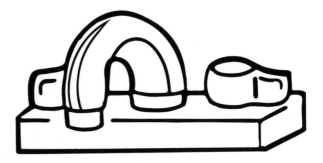

Faucet

Turn off the faucet while brushing your teeth.

Recycle Bin

Paper, plastic, and aluminum garbage goes into the recycle bin. (Check first with a parent or caregiver!)

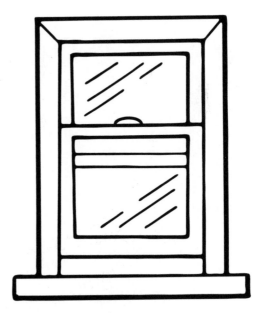

Window

Close the windows when the heat or air conditioning is on.

Arbor Day

The last Friday in April is Arbor Day. On this day, people are encouraged to plant trees. Why? Because trees provide cleaner air, food for animals and people, shade on hot days, natural beauty, and more.

On this page, color in the oak, palm, and evergreen trees.

On the right-hand page, color and cut out the shapes to make your own evergreen tree and apple tree.

Oak

Palm

Evergreen

Get a Jump on It

Hop to it, and connect dots 1 through 61. Color the picture when you're done.

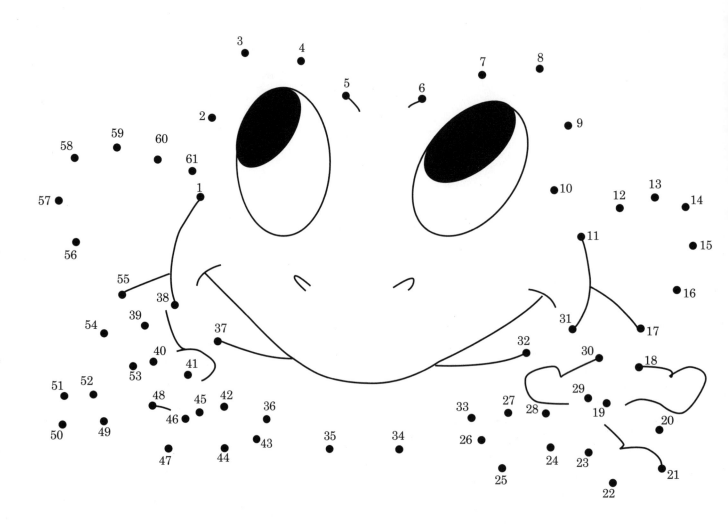

Answer on page 96.

Days to Celebrate

Happy Mother's Day!

Cinco de Mayo

On Cinco de Mayo (May 5), Mexican heritage and pride are celebrated.

On this page, color and cut out the sombrero and maracas, two symbols of Mexican culture. On the right-hand page, color the outfits of the children, who are dressed up for Cinco de Mayo.

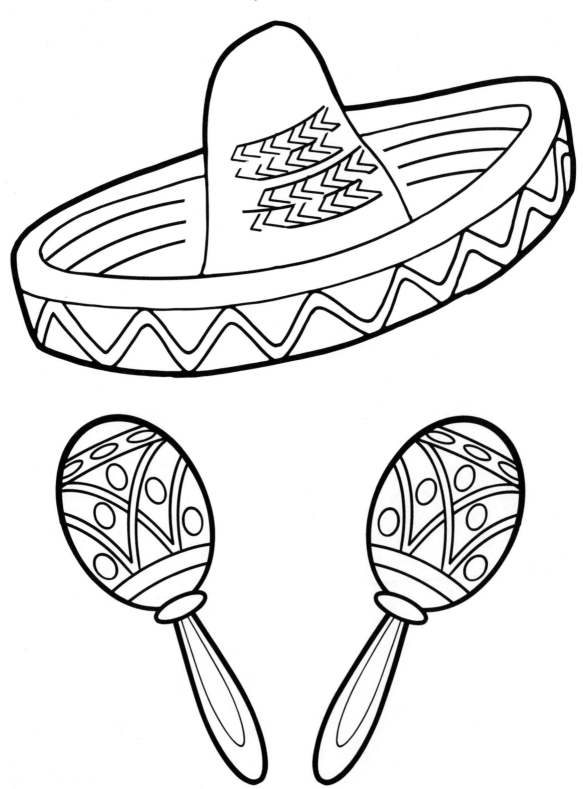

To the Moon!

Are you ready to build a three-dimensional rocket ship? It's easy. First, color the pieces of the rocket ship. Cut out the patterns. Turn the pattern below into a cylinder, securing it with glue or tape. Cut slits along the straight lines of the cylinder and the fins, and insert the fins. Turn the semicircle pattern into the cone-shaped top of the rocket. Prepare for blastoff!

finished project

Mother's Day Card

Why buy a Mother's Day card when you can make one yourself?
Cut out the card's cover and interior pages. Paste the pages on the
back of the card, and fold. Color the cover. On the writing lines,
list all the things you love about your mom or caregiver.

What I Love About Mom

Mother's Day Coupons

Here is a gift that Mom is sure to love! Cut out these coupons and present them to your mother or caregiver. You might want to include them in a Mother's Day card. Be sure you live up to your promises!

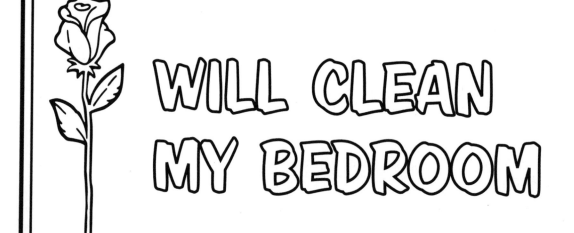

WILL CLEAN MY BEDROOM

ONE DAY OF BEST BEHAVIOR

WILL HELP WASH DISHES

WILL TAKE OUT TRASH

WILL READ A BOOK TOGETHER

A Picture to Cherish

Find a great photo of you and your mom or caregiver. Cut out the middle of this frame, and paste or tape the photo to the back of the frame. Once you color it, you'll have a great Mother's Day gift!

Mom and Me

Choo-Choo!

National Train Day is celebrated every May.
Color and cut out this classic train engine.

A Good Day for a Picnic

With the weather warming up, May is a pleasant time to enjoy a picnic. You can have a pretend picnic in the classroom. Color and cut out these pictures and the picnic basket, and place the items in the basket.

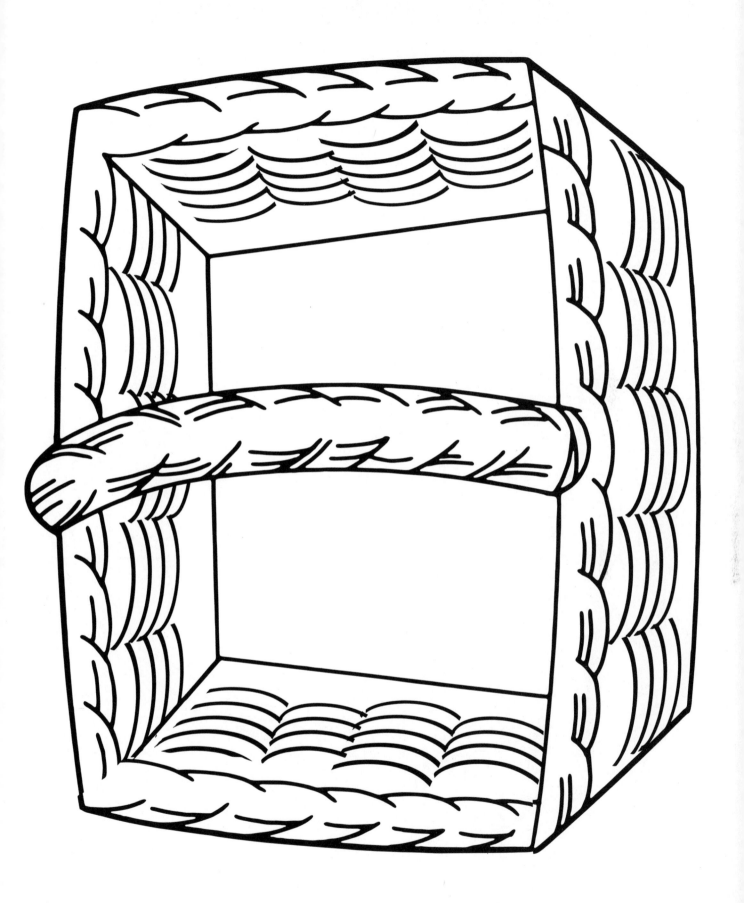

Be Kind to Animals

Be Kind to Animals Week is celebrated in early May. Color this barnyard scene. Be sure to give a pat on the head to the horse, donkey, sheep, duck, rabbit, and goat!

Amusement Park

You won't need a ticket to visit this wacky amusement park! Test your powers of observation by completing the following activities. Don't use the same answer twice.

1. Find 5 things that begin with the letter *R*.

2. Find 3 long, thin things hidden in this picture.

3. Find 5 other things that don't belong in an amusement park.

Answers on page 96.

Make a Book

Reading Is Fun Week is celebrated each May. Here is your chance to write something fun. Write a poem that rhymes and a poem that is just plain silly! Cut out the cover and the pages, and then paste them together to create your own book.

My Book of Fun Poems

By _____

Published by Rhyme Time, Inc.

Silly Poem

Rhyming Poem

Fluttering Butterflies

With crayons and creativity, you can make these butterflies beautiful! When you are done coloring, cut out the butterflies and punch smalls holes in the top-middle of each. Hang the butterflies from a hanger with thread or string. Watch them flutter!

Pizza Party!

National Pizza Party Day, held every May, is a great reason to
celebrate. Color and cut out the pizza as well as the toppings.
Then place your favorite toppings on your pizza. Delicious!

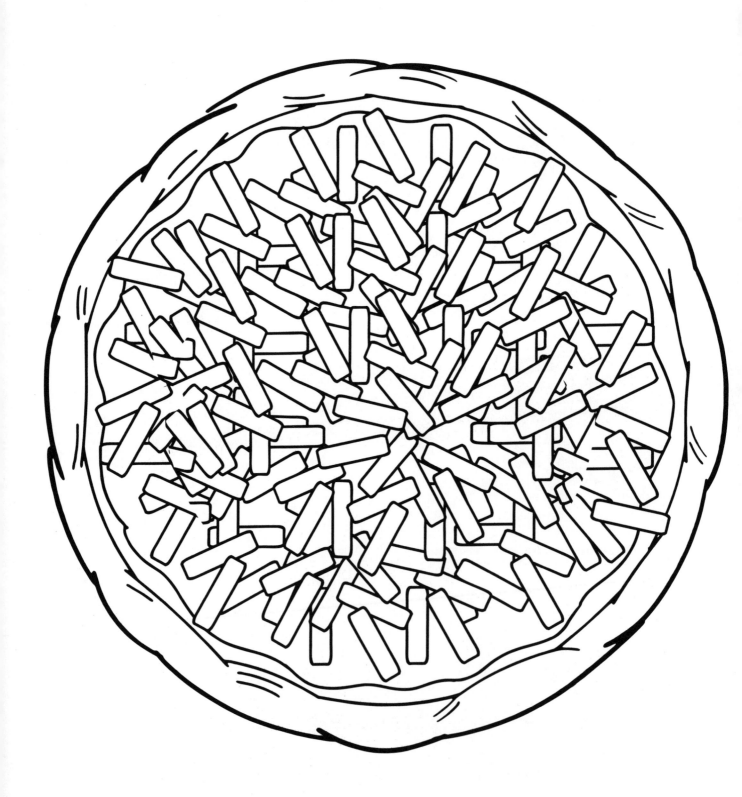

Pepperoni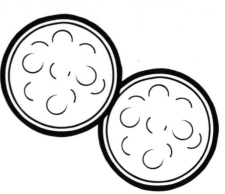

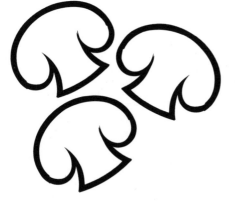 **Mushrooms**

Tomato

 **Onion**

Pineapple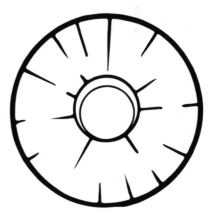

 **Spinach leaves**

Baseball Birthday

By coloring the stitches red, you can create a birthday badge that looks like a baseball. Write your name and birthday on the lines. Wear the badge with pride!

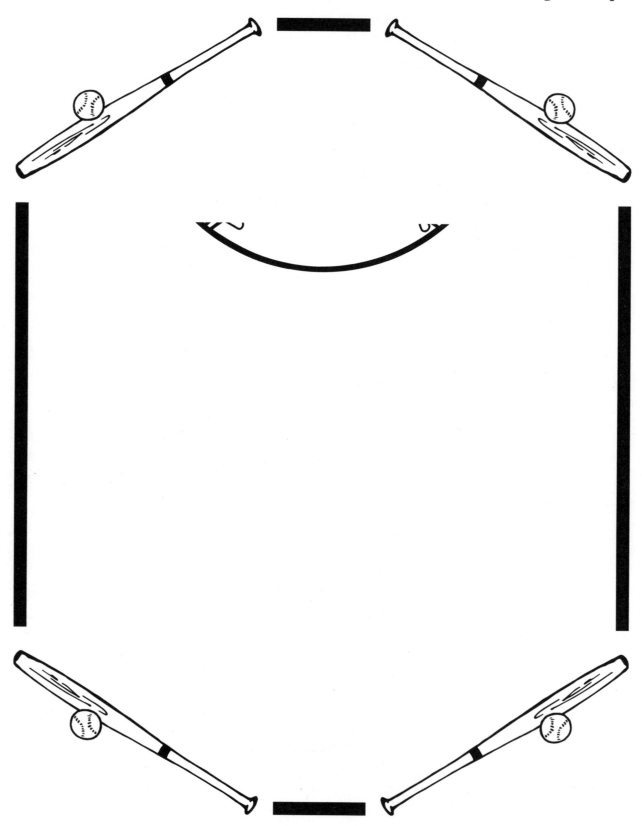

Zoom! Zoom! Zoom!

The Indianapolis 500 auto race is run on the day before Memorial Day. Color and cut out this cool Indy-style racecar.

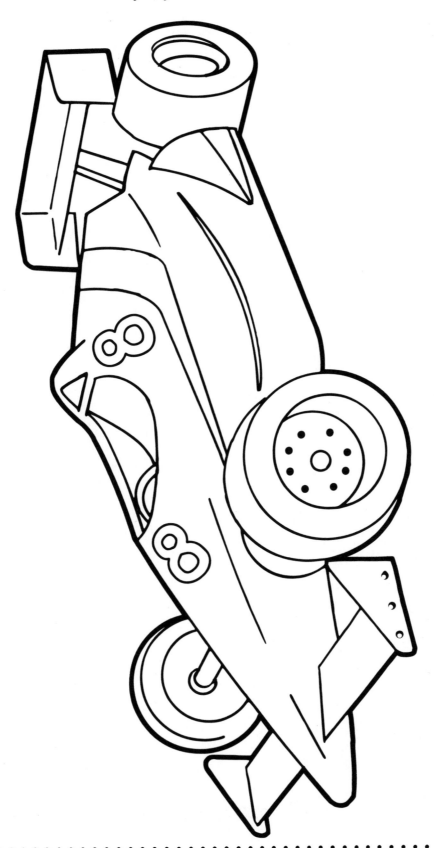

Prepare a Police Officer

National Police Week is celebrated every May. It is a great time to honor our country's police officers. They often put themselves in harm's way to protect us. In this fun activity, you get to prepare the police officers. Color and cut out their clothes and accessories. Use the flaps to fasten the clothes onto the officers' bodies. The accessories can be glued or taped.

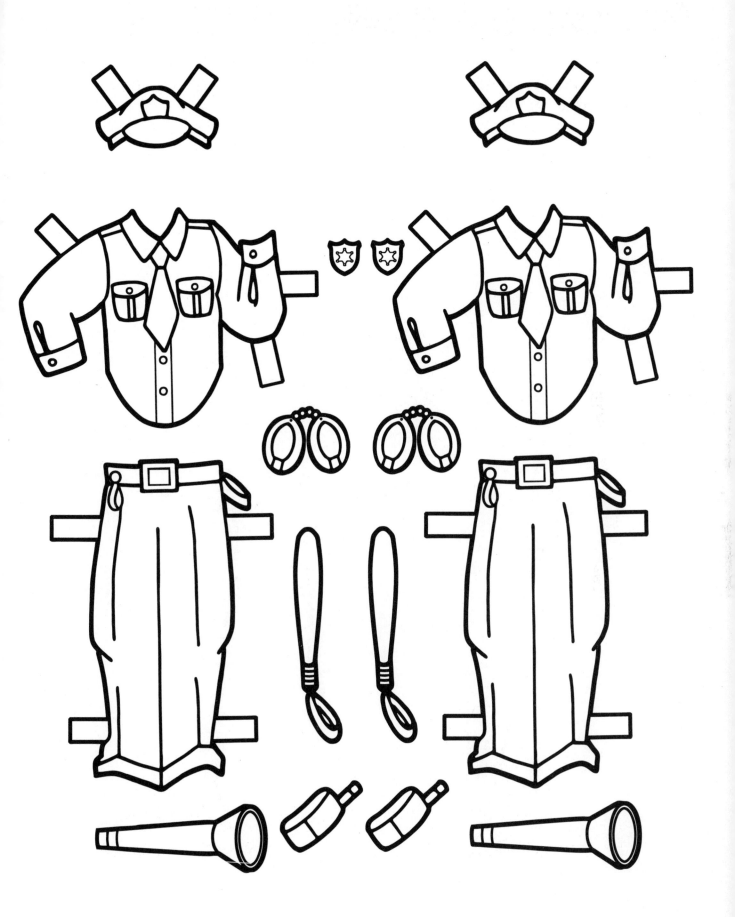

Memorial Day

Memorial Day is held on the last Monday in May. On this special holiday, we honor the American men and women who have died while serving in the military. In many communities, parades are held on this day.

Color and cut out the flag below. You can display it in the classroom or bring it home with you. On the right-hand page, color the servicewoman and serviceman, who are marching on Memorial Day.

Answers

Bee-lieve It! *(page 14)*

March Madness
(pages 18–19)
The home team's total is 36.

Slow Movin'
(page 21)

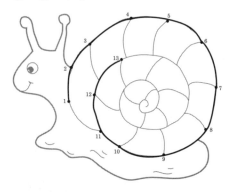

Home Fixes *(page 27)*
1. car; 2. chimney;
3. doorknob; 4. jump rope; 5. lawnmower's wheels; 6. missing "5";
7. tree's leaves; 8. wagon's handles; 9. water from hose; 10. weather vane (to name a few).

Flower Power
(page 31)

Springtime Crossword *(page 36)*

It's Raining, It's Pouring *(page 45)*

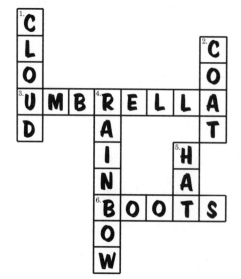

Easter Egg Hunt
(page 54)

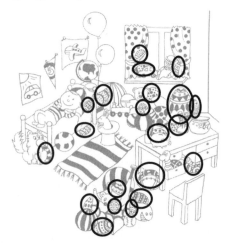

Count and Color Jellybeans *(page 55)*
The total number of jelly beans is 56.

Get a Jump on It
(page 66)

Amusement Park
(page 83)
1. These start with R: radio, ruler, rabbit, ring, rake.
2. These are hidden: pencil, baseball bat, spoon.
3. These don't belong: cow on Ferris wheel, lawn mower, chair, frying pan, telephone.

TEACHERS' FAVORITES™

Fun Activities for SUMMER!

Reproducible Patterns for
Paper Crafts, Coloring Pages, Games,
Decorations, and More!

Illustrations by Rick Ewigleben

Publications International, Ltd.

Introduction written by Holli Fort.

Contents

Beat the Heat with Cool Summer Fun!

It's easy enough to color a smiling sun or cut out a surfboard. But having inventive and engaging activities that students respond to, have fun with, and maybe even learn from can be a daunting task. This is true whether you lead a classroom, Sunday school class, scout troop, or a home filled with eager learners. The adaptable projects featured in *Teachers' Favorites*™: *Fun Activities for Summer!* will help you challenge your students with educational activities and purely fun seasonal projects.

Each season in this four-book series offers up a unique buffet of holidays, milestones, sports, and activities. Summer is the time for Father's Day, Independence Day, camping, volleyball, and stargazing. Students will enjoy relevant crafts that can be hung, worn, read, laminated, given as gifts, or used to decorate the room or bulletin board.

Teachers' Favorites™: *Fun Activities for Summer!* includes the following types of activities:

• Coloring
• Writing
• Math
• Paper crafts
• Games, such as look-and-find, connect the dots, and mazes

For craft projects, take the time to go over the instructions carefully. Also, make sure you have all the materials on hand before you get started. Here are just a few of the materials that are required for most projects:

Paper: Since the projects in this book will need to be photocopied for each student, be sure to have plenty of paper. Most projects can be copied on regular copy paper, but some projects (such as paper dolls and cutouts that stand) should be copied on heavier stock or construction paper. If you do not have access to heavier stock or your copier cannot accommodate construction paper, you can glue the project's paper to construction paper to make it sturdier. For some projects, such as the card for Father's Day, it is important that you can't see through the paper. In such cases, you might want to glue construction paper to the back of the paper.

Glue and tape: Some projects call for glue and/or clear tape. If you use glue, make sure it is water-base and nontoxic.

Scissors: Many projects call for cutting out pieces. Some require cutting slits or poking holes. For younger children, you may need to do the cutting yourself—or have older children help. Always have safety scissors around for smaller hands!

Brads: Some projects call for brass brads to hold pieces together. If you do not have those on hand, you can substitute with twist ties.

Art supplies: Children can use crayons, markers, or paint to color these projects. If children will be painting, be aware that acrylic paint will dry permanently, though when wet it is easily cleaned up with water. Make sure children clean painting tools thoroughly when they are finished painting.

Art smock: Make sure children wear smocks or old shirts to protect clothes while working with paints and other messy materials.

Flex Time

Another great thing about the crafts, coloring pages, and writing pages in this book is that they provide for versatility—which definitely comes in handy when working with children of

differing skill levels. The crafts can be simplified or made more complex depending on need.

Coloring pages are simple enough for younger children, but older children may want to challenge themselves by adding patterns, textures, or even decorations. Likewise, the writing pages are great for older children to let their imaginations flow in creating original stories, while beginning writers may use them to copy a few words or dictate longer stories to an adult. If your group is of mixed ages, consider taking a teamwork approach that combines the imaginative approach of a younger child and the writing skills of an older child.

Great Clips

Clip-art pages are great for all kinds of applications. You can use a copy machine to increase the size of the seasonal images to make them suitable for wall or bulletin board decorations. Likewise, you can use the copier to make images smaller for use on worksheets, bulletins, notes to parents, or any other application you can dream up. Incorporate the clip-art images to create seasonal birthday cards or stationery, or use them to add a decorative element to any other project.

In the Mix

All of the projects presented in this book, from the simplest to the most elaborate, are just ideas to get you started. Feel free to alter the designs by choosing different materials or embellishing in any number of unique ways. Give your imagination free rein as you play around with materials and these base ideas. Encourage students to come up with their own unique variations on these themes, and keep them in mind for later uses. You can jump off in any direction, keeping these projects as fun and fresh as the first time you tried them. When it comes to creating fun summertime activities, the sky is the limit!

Summertime Bugs!

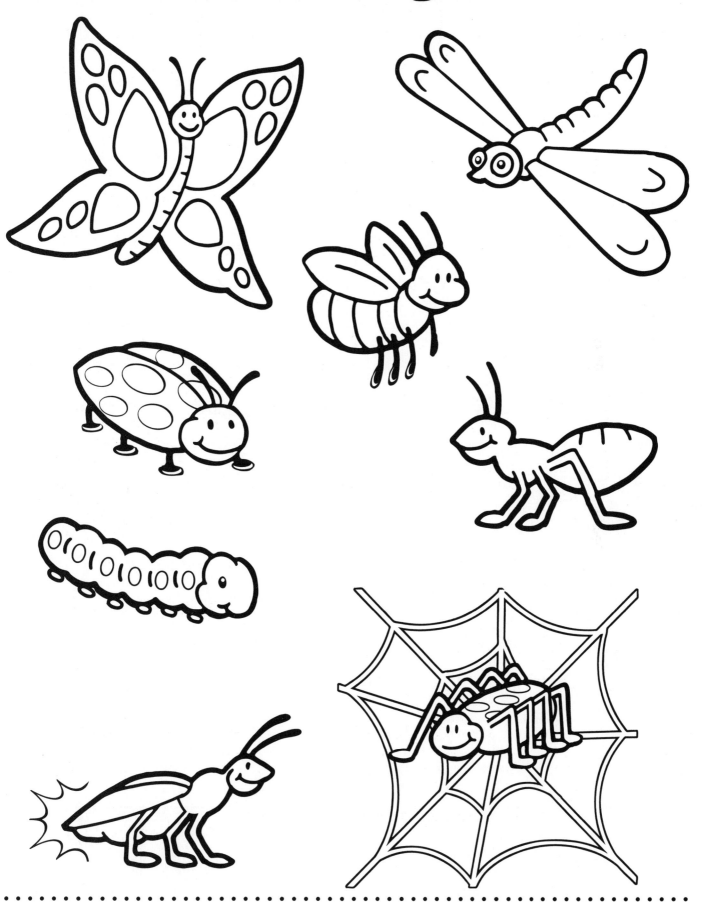

Special June Days

Special June Days

A Birthday Hat

Celebrate this month's birthdays with this fun hat. Color, cut out, and tape or glue the hat. Then use a piece of string to secure the hat around your chin.

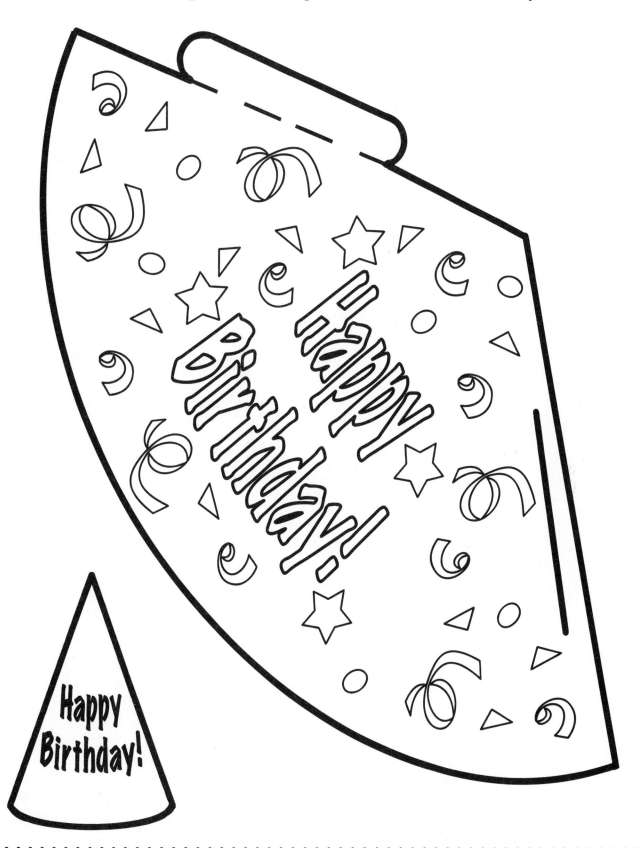

It's National Smile Month!

Something is missing from the face on this page. Can you color and cut out the face and the smiles and make sure the person is happy? Try putting each of the smiles on the face to pick your favorite!

It's National Smile Month!

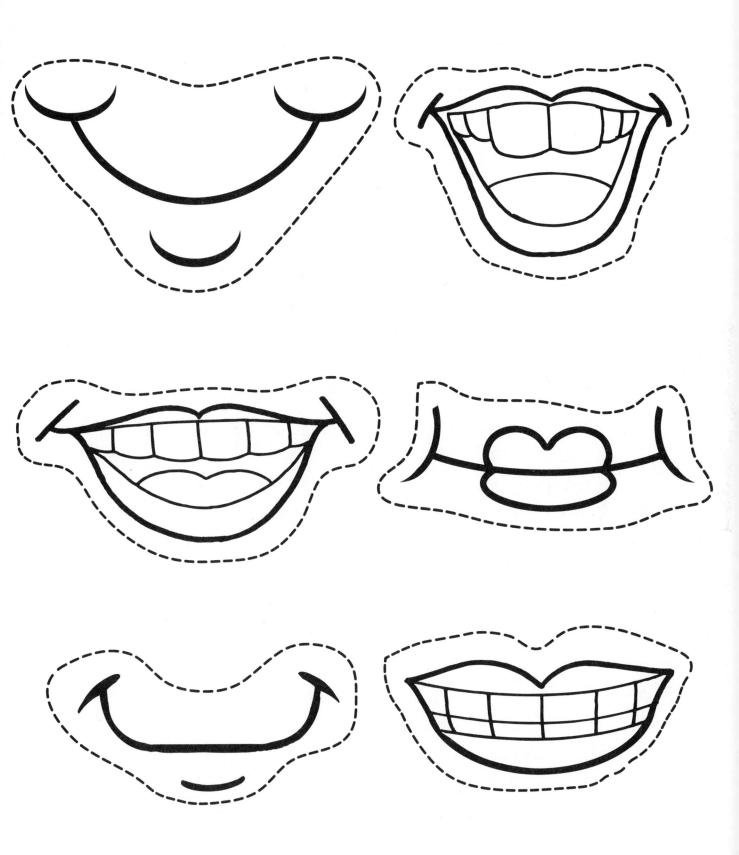

Web Site

Help the little bug cross the spiderwebs and avoid the spiders.

START

FINISH

Answer on page 96.

Donut Day!

Donuts are a neat breakfast treat. In June, you can celebrate Donut Day to honor this fun food. Make this donut delicious by coloring and decorating it. Paste on some glitter or confetti to add some scrumptious sprinkles!

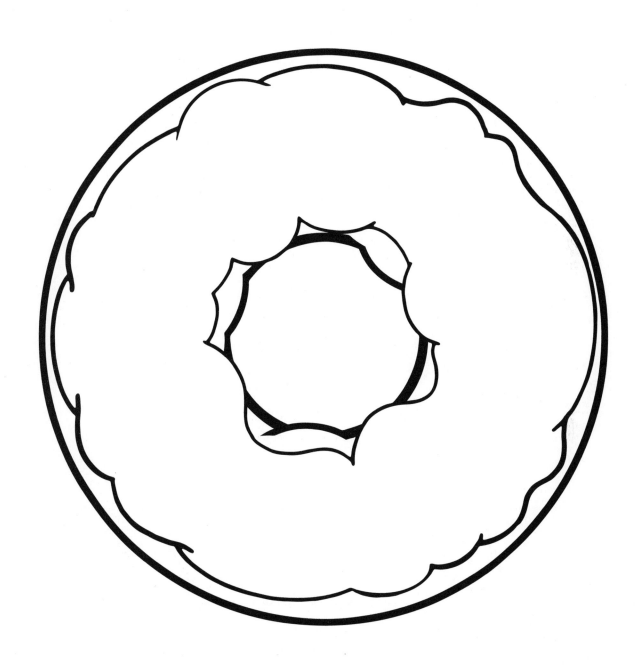

What I Learned This Year

Write about something fun or interesting you learned in school this year.

_____

_____

_____

_____

_____

_____

_____

_____

_____

_____

_____

End of School Diploma

Congratulations!

has completed _____ grade!

Let's Play Soccer!

Soccer is a fun game to play outside. Now you can play inside, too! Color, cut out, and put together the soccer players and the goal. Make a soccer ball out of crumpled-up scrap paper, and use the dolls to "kick" the ball into the goal. If you want, you can make two goals and challenge a friend to play against you!

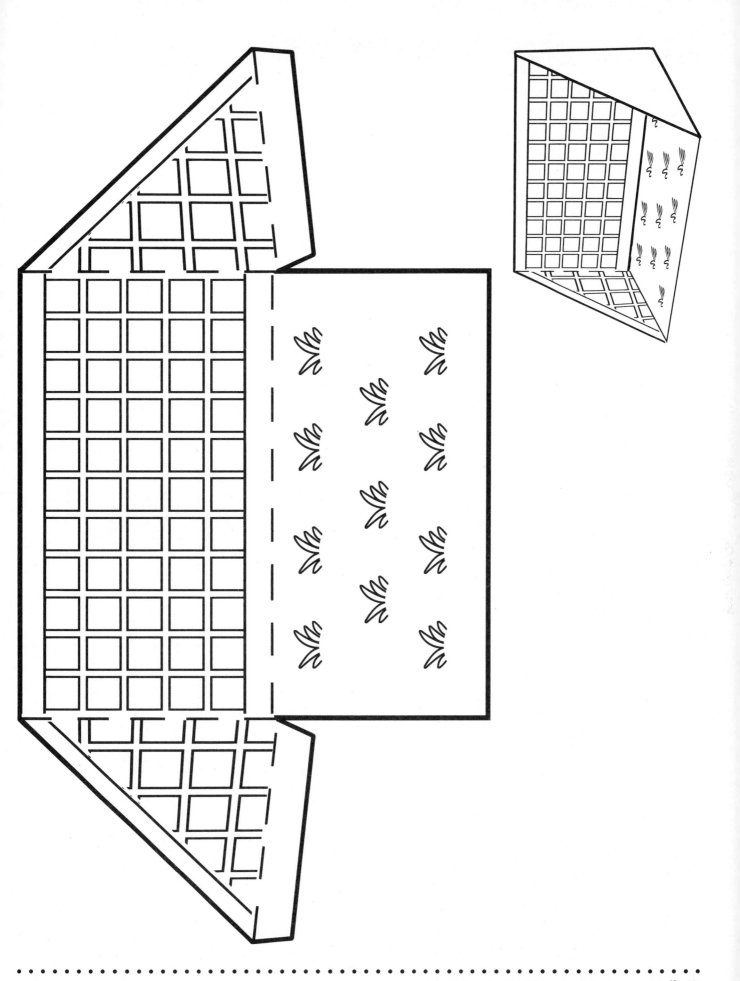

Why My Dad Is Special

Write something special about your father. You can also write about a grandfather or uncle.

_____

_____

_____

_____

_____

_____

_____

_____

_____

A Father's Day Card

Here is a Father's Day card you can color, decorate, and give to your dad or someone special! You can write a message or draw a picture inside of the card.

A Father's Day Ribbon

This is a special prize to let your dad know how special he is to you! Decorate it with your dad's favorite colors. On the strands of the ribbon, write words that tell why your dad is special.

It's National Candy Month

June is National Candy Month! To celebrate, you can color and cut out these pieces of candy. Thread a ribbon or string through the candy ends to make your own candy necklace.

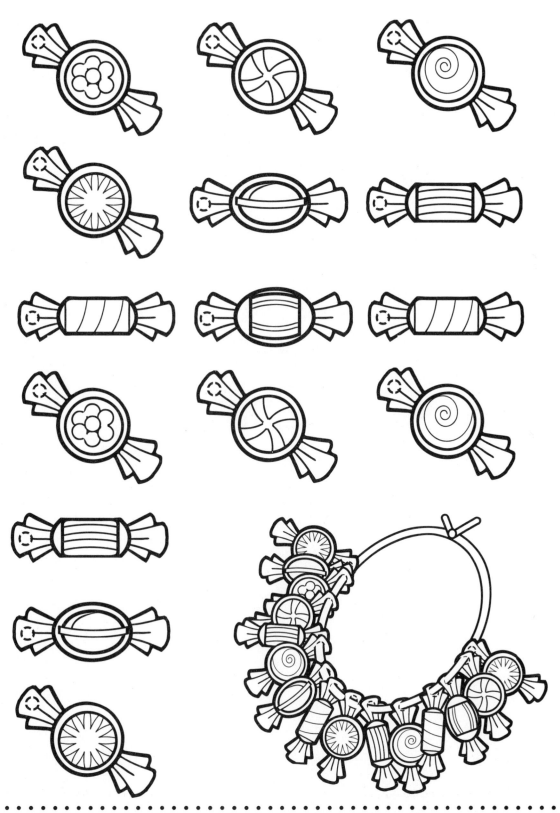

Whose Kite Am I?

What a windy day! These four friends were just in the park, flying their kites, when a huge gust of wind tangled the strings. Can you figure out which kite belongs to which person? (Be careful! The kite strings will cross each other.)

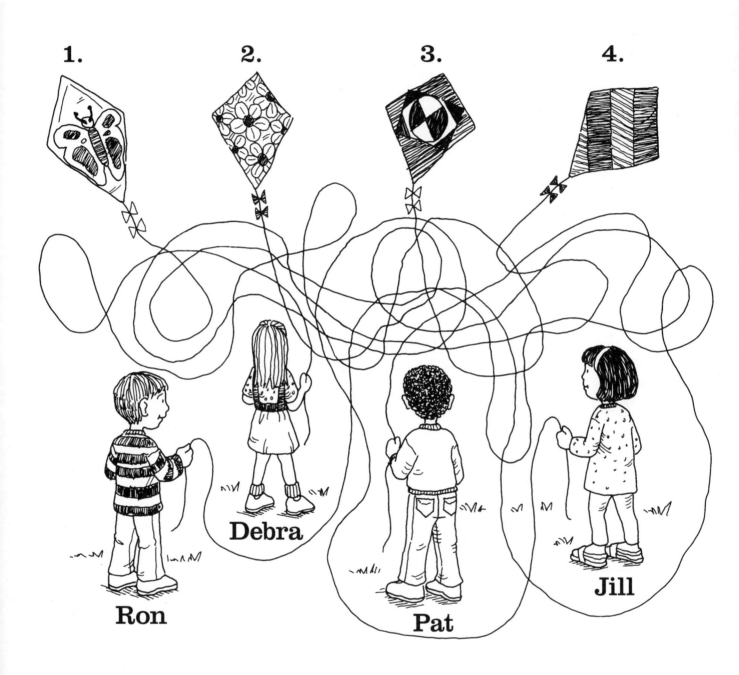

1.

2.

3.

4.

Debra

Ron

Pat

Jill

Answers on page 96.

It's Flag Day!

Every June 14 we honor the American flag with Flag Day. Color this flag so it's ready to fly for Flag Day!

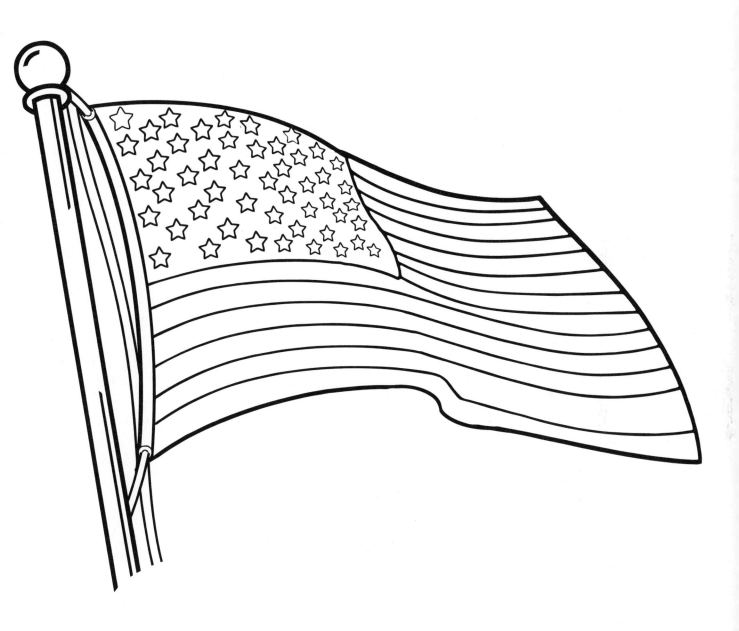

Build a Bicycle

Get ready to bike! Color and cut out the pieces of the bicycle. Then, attach the wheels to the frame of the bicycle. If you have them, use metal fasteners so the wheels of the bicycle can spin. You can also use tape or glue, if you like.

My Picnic Story

Write a story about a fun picnic you have enjoyed. You can also make up a fun picnic story!

_____

_____

_____

_____

_____

_____

_____

_____

_____

_____

A Big Barbecue

Something sure smells good! Color and cut out the grill and all of the food so you can cook up your favorite barbecue treats.

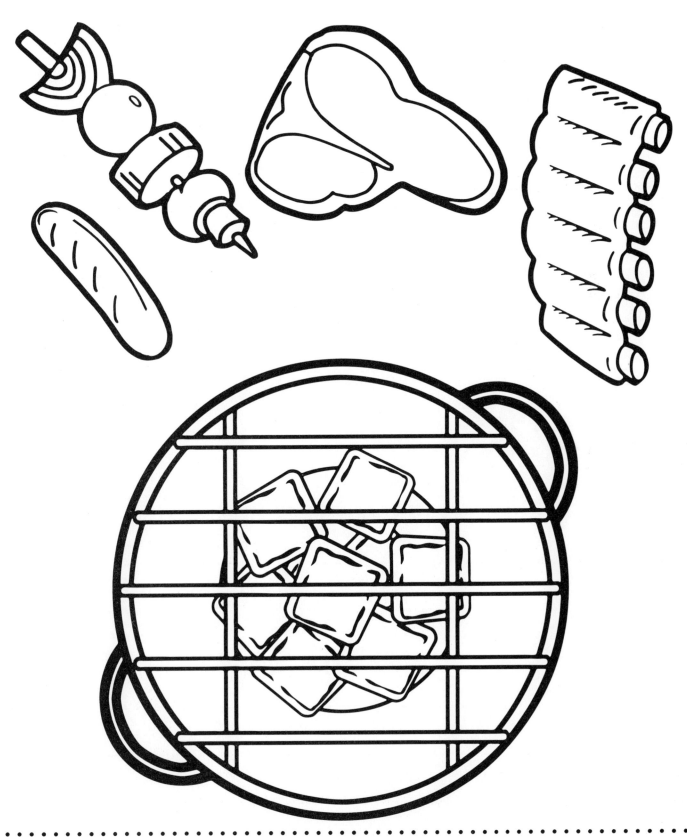

That's One Tasty Burger!

This hamburger looks delicious, but you have to put it together before you can eat it! Color and cut out the hamburger, bun, and toppings. Then, stack everything up to build your own tasty burger.

A Summer Storm

Summer has lots of sunny days, but sometimes it can be cloudy and rainy. Once in a while, the weather gets really wild and you get big storms with thunder and lightning! Color and cut out these clouds, lightning bolts, and rain gear. Create your own rainy day display!

Get Ready to Fish!

This boy and girl are getting ready to go fishing. Help them prepare by coloring and decorating their clothes. After you finish coloring, cut out the boy and girl.

Let's Go Fishing!

It's time to get a line in the water and go fishing! Color the fish and the pond, then cut them out. Tape or glue paper clips to the backs of the fish and lay them in the pond. Then, tie a piece of string to the end of a pencil and attach the other end of the string to a small magnet to make your own fishing pole. Use the fishing dolls that you made before with your new fishing pole to catch the fish!

Splish Splash

Can you find the 17 differences between the top and the bottom pool scenes?

Answers on page 96.

Summer Vacation!

The 4th of July

A Birthday Certificate

Celebrate this month's birthdays with this fun certificate. Color and cut out the certificate, and then write your name on the line if you have a July birthday!

Happy Birthday!

_____

is ___ years old today!

It's National Hot Dog Month!

Did you know that July is National Hot Dog Month? You can join in the fun by decorating this hot dog stand! Write your name on the sign and draw yourself working. You can write the menu and draw hot dogs or other foods you like, too!

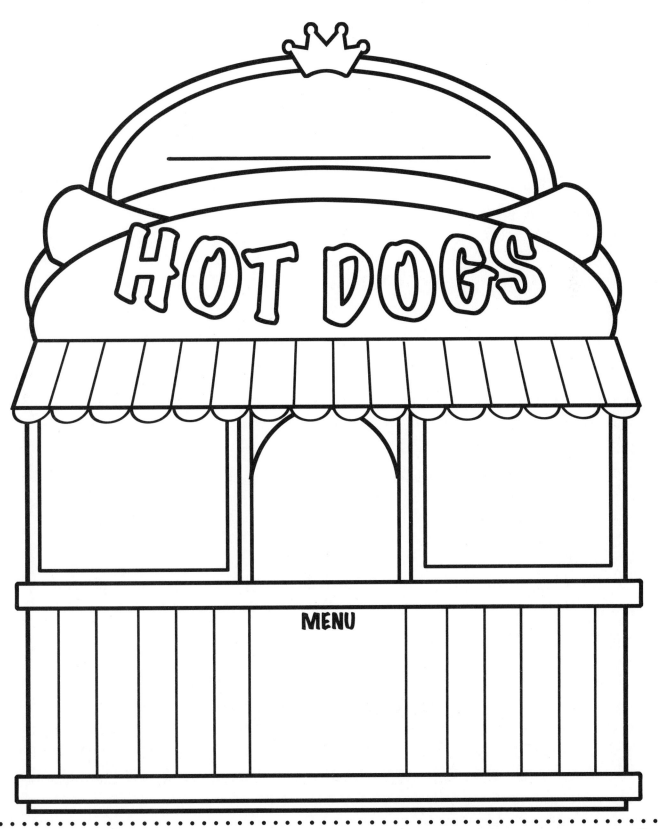

Mighty Monument

Below is one of the most popular monuments in the United States. See if you can finish the monument by connecting the dots 1 through 18.

Answer on page 96.

My 4th of July

How do you like to celebrate the 4th of July? Write about something you like to do on this holiday.

_____

_____

_____

_____

_____

_____

_____

_____

_____

_____

U.S. Postage Stamp Day

July 1 is U.S. Postage Stamp Day! Stamps have all kinds of pictures on them. What would you like to see on a stamp? In the outline you can draw a special stamp to honor somebody you think is a hero or just somebody you like a lot!

Watch the Fireworks!

Do you know what else happens on the 4th of July? Fireworks! In the sky below, use colorful crayons or markers to make your own exciting fireworks display.

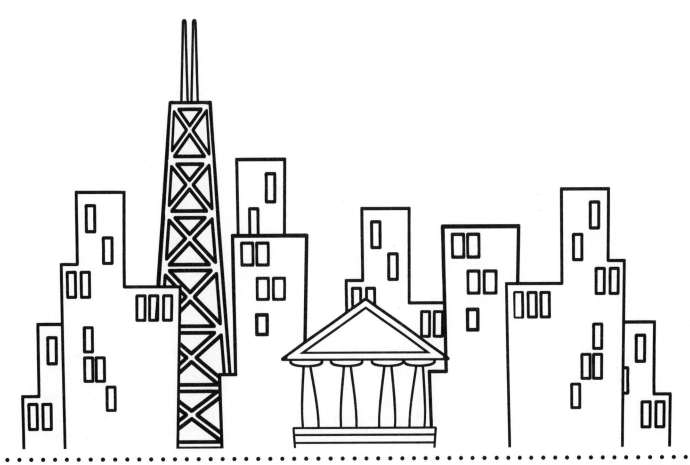

The 4th of July Parade!

Lots of people go see parades to celebrate the 4th of July. Color and cut out all of the pictures below. You can then arrange your own parade!

A Beach Puzzle!

Prepare to be puzzled! Color the picture below, and cut it into the pieces of a jigsaw puzzle. Mix up the pieces, and then put the picture back together again!

A Day at the Beach

This beach looks empty! Can you bring everyone back to the beach? Draw and color some people, animals, boats, toys, and whatever else you would like to see at the beach!

Fun in the Water and Sun!

Write about a fun trip you would like to take to a beach, pool, or water park.

_____

_____

_____

_____

_____

_____

_____

_____

_____

_____

_____

It's National Ice Cream Month!

July is National Ice Cream Month! Nothing beats a cool treat on a hot summer day. Color and cut out the cone and ice cream scoops. Try to decorate the scoops so they look like your favorite ice cream flavors! Add sprinkles in your favorite colors.

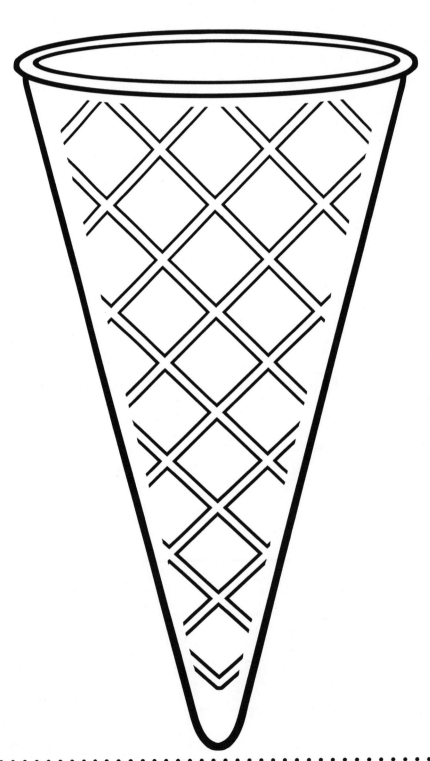

Wild Wally's Water Park

Jump on an inner tube, and slide through the maze to the tropical lagoon.

Answer on page 96.

A Trip to the Ballpark

Write about a baseball game that you have played or watched. You can also write about another sport that you enjoy!

Summer Sports

Summer is a great time to go outside and play sports. Color and cut out the boy and girl and their clothes. Dress them so they're ready to play your favorite summer sport! Then try all of the other clothes!

Summer Flowers

One of the best things about summer is all of the beautiful flowers! Color and cut out the flowers and flowerpot. Add straws or pipe cleaners to the backs of the flowers to make stems. Then, use tape or glue to arrange all of your flowers in the flowerpot!

Cows and Cowboys!

Did you know that July 25 is Cow Appreciation Day and National Day of the Cowboy? Celebrate this fun day by coloring and cutting out the cows, cowboy, and fences. Hang the pieces with string to make a neat mobile!

It's Picnic Time!

This family looks like it's ready to dig in and enjoy a picnic, but something is missing! Can you draw and color a tasty picnic lunch for them? You can draw all of your favorite picnic foods!

Starry Night

Summer nights are a great time to go outside and look up at the stars. Color and cut out all of the pictures below. Arrange and paste them all on a black piece of paper to make your own starry night scene. Then you can stargaze any time you like!

Pack for Your Trip!

Many people spend their summer vacation by going on a trip. You can't travel until you pack your bags! Color and decorate the stickers with words or pictures that tell about a place you have been or somewhere you would like to go. Color the suitcase, and cut everything out. Tape or glue the stickers on your suitcase, and get ready to hit the road!

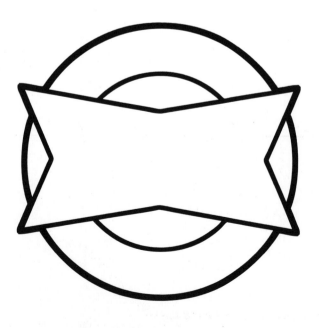
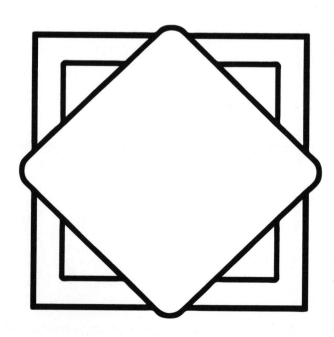

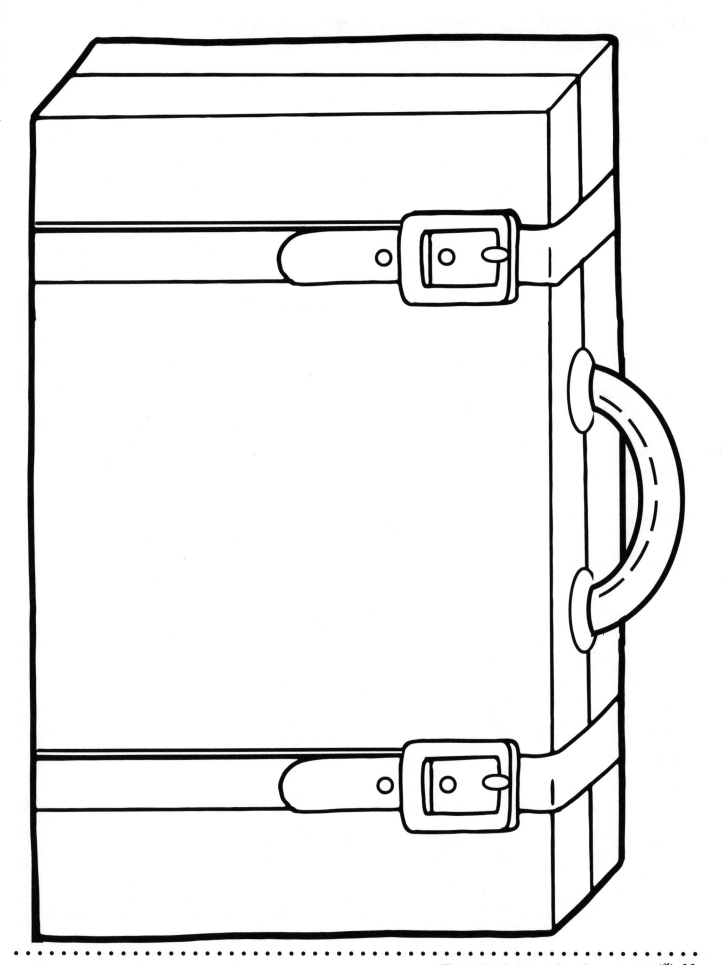

Going on Vacation!

Going on vacation is fun! Write about a trip you have taken or would like to take.

It's a Hot One Today

All ten words in the word list are hidden in the sun-shape grid below. Look across, down, and diagonally to find these words about the weather. Circle each word in the grid as you find it, and then cross it off the word list. We circled *WET* to get you started.

CLOUDY   SLEET

DAMP   STORM

HAIL   THUNDER

HOT   ~~WET~~

LIGHTNING   WIND

```
              S
S             L             U
   N        W E T        R
      H A E H I
   N A S T O R M
T O L I G H T N I N G
   C L O U D Y R
      W I N D A
   N     A D D     M
O        E         P
         R
```

Answers on page 96.

August

Summer Fun!

Summer Fun!

Let's Go Camping!

A Magical Birthday!

Celebrate this month's birthdays with this fun birthday wand. Color and cut out the wand for everyone with an August birthday!

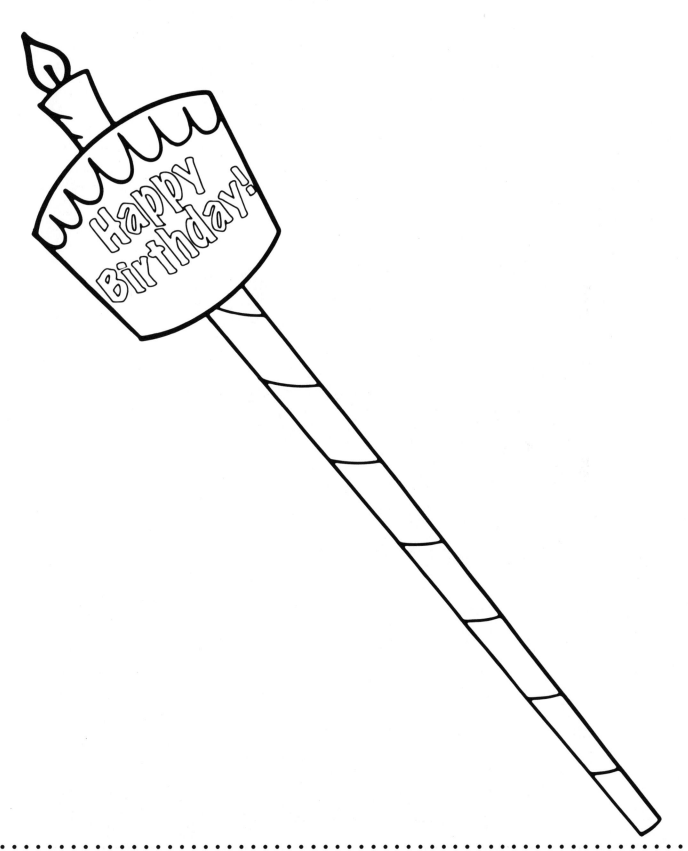

Waffle Week!

Did you know that the first week of August is Waffle Week? Color and cut out the waffle and toppings, and then put them all together. If you don't see your favorite topping, you can draw it yourself!

A Sunny Day Seek

Can you find these 13 items hidden in the picture?

Answers on page 96.

How I Beat the Heat!

Write about something you do to stay cool in the summertime.

_____

_____

_____

_____

_____

_____

_____

_____

_____

_____

Build a Lighthouse

August 7 is Lighthouse Day! Celebrate this fun day by making your own lighthouse. Color and cut out the pieces on the next page, and then attach the buildings to this island with tape or glue.

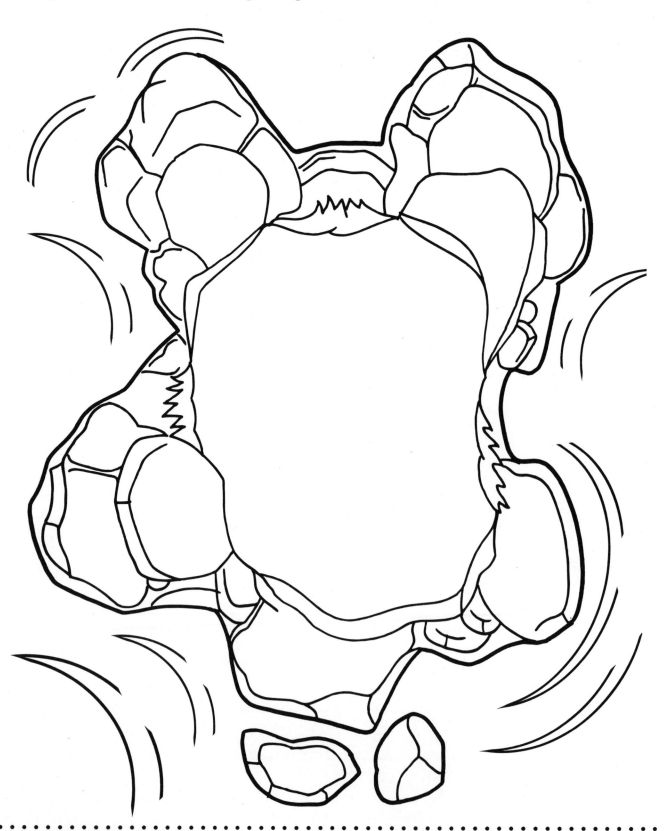

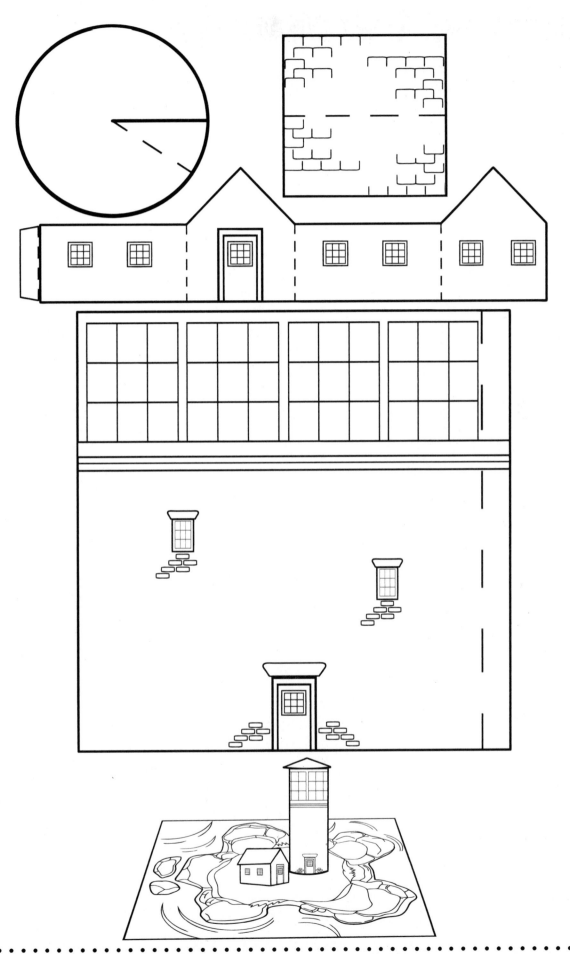

Pairs of Twins!

Did you know that August 7 is also Twins Day? Color the children, and help each set of twins find one another by drawing a line connecting them. You can also cut them out and match them up, if you like!

Time to Play!

The playground is a fun place to go in the summer! Color the playground, and draw you and your friends playing on your favorite playground equipment!

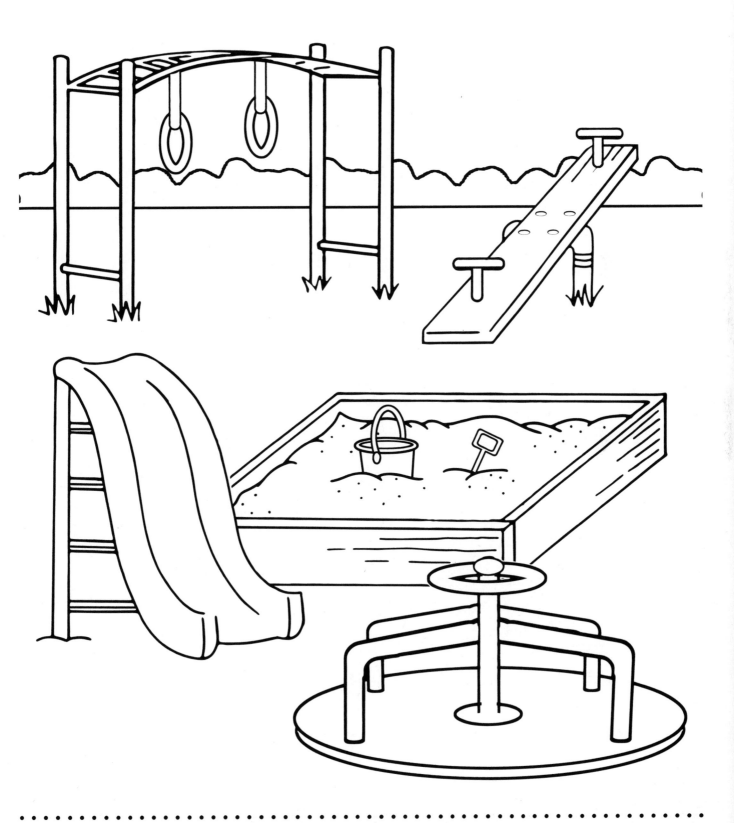

Volleyball Fun!

Volleyball is a great game to play at the beach or in your own backyard! Color and cut out the volleyball players and their net. Set up the net, and use a small ball of scrap paper to play volleyball whenever you want!

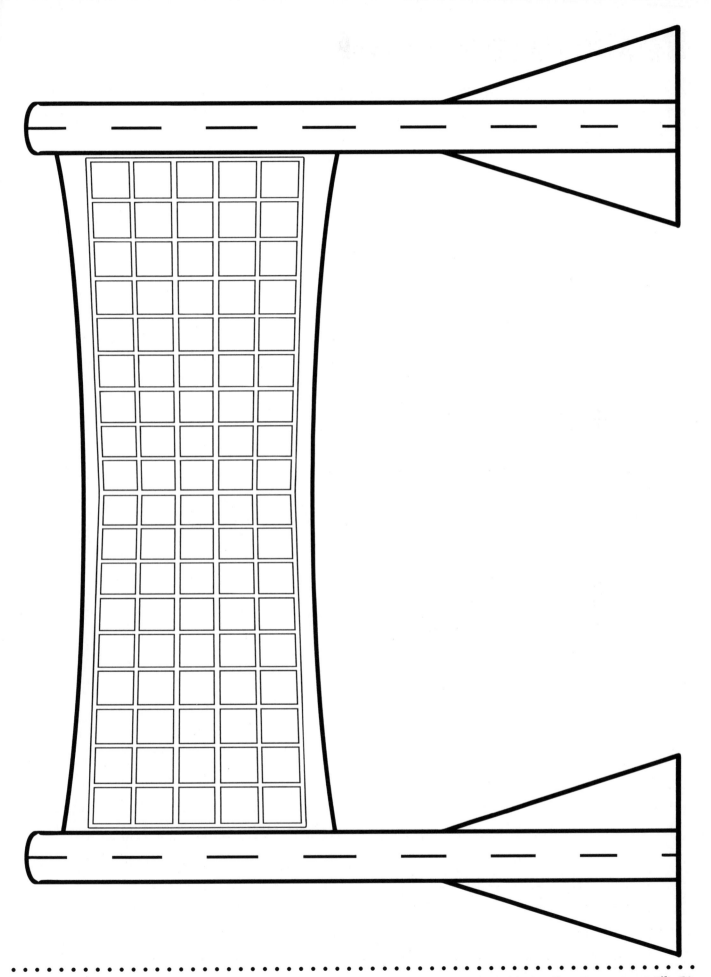

What a Sunny Day!

There's nothing better than a nice, sunny day! Now you can enjoy the best things about a sunny day all the time! Color and cut out all of the sunny day pictures below. String them all together to make your own sunny day display!

What I Like to Do Outside

Write about your favorite things to do outside during the summer.

_____

_____

_____

_____

_____

_____

_____

_____

_____

· · · · · · · **What I Like to Do Outside** · · · · · · · ·

It's Cupcake Day!

August 18 is Cupcake Day! To celebrate, cut out and decorate the cupcake. You can color it and attach some fun sprinkles or glitter with glue!

Sunny Day

Pull out your crayons or markers. Color the circles yellow, the squares blue, the triangles red, and the rectangles green. Fill in the rest of the scene with whatever colors you want.

Write a Postcard!

It's fun to send and receive postcards! Decorate the postcard, and write a note to a friend about somewhere you went this summer or something fun you did. Once you finish both sides of the postcard, you can tape or glue them together with a piece of card stock in the middle. Ask a grown-up for help if you'd like to mail it!

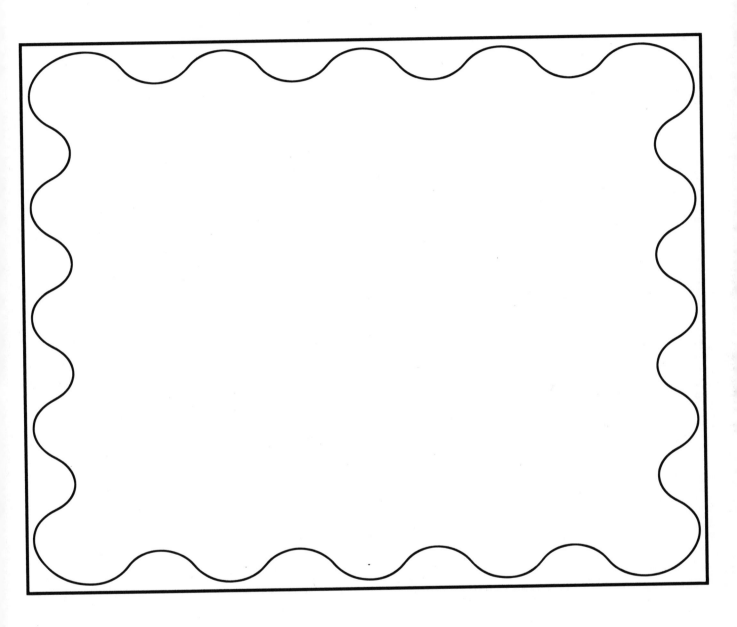

Gather Around the Campfire

Summer is a great time to go camping. When people go camping, they build campfires to cook food and stay warm at night. Color and decorate the campfire and the campfire items. Then you can cut out the campfire items and add them to the scene around the fire!

In My Tent!

You can't go camping without a tent! Inside the tent, draw you and a friend or relative you would like to go with you on a camping trip.

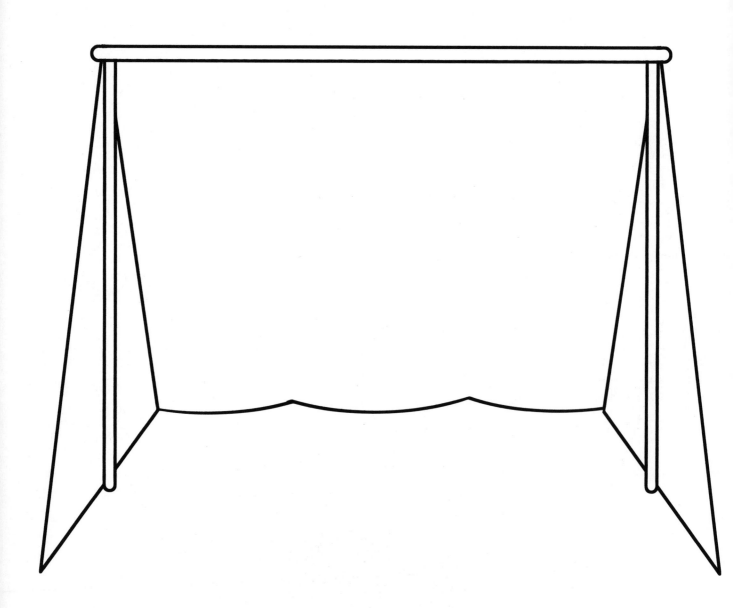

Fan the Heat Away

Fans help people stay cool during the summer. Decorate the fan with a fun drawing or design. Attach a wooden stick, pencil, or plastic straw to use as a handle.

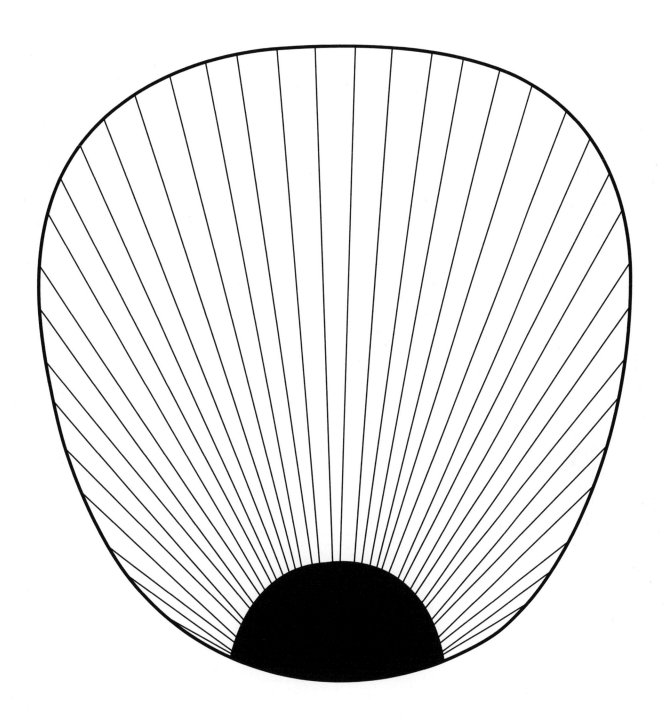

My Amazing Invention!

Write about something you could invent to make life better for everyone!

_____

_____

_____

_____

_____

_____

_____

_____

_____

_____

_____

My Best Friend!

Did you know that part of August is Friendship Week? In the frame, draw a picture of what you and your best friend like to do when you are together!

A Cool Pair of Shades!

Keep the summer sun out of your eyes with your own pair of sunglasses! Color and cut out the parts of the sunglasses, and glue or tape them together. If you have some colored cellophane, use it to make lenses for your shades!

Fruit Salad

All eight fruits in the word list are hidden in the berry-shape grid below. Look across, down, and diagonally. Circle each word in the grid as you find it, and cross it off the word list. We circled *BANANA* to get you started.

~~BANANA~~   ORANGE
BERRY   PEACH
GRAPE   PEAR
MELON   PLUM

```
        H I
            O
            R
      P E A C H
    G B A N A N A
    G E P G N P E
    C R M E L O N
    T R A U A A R
    Y M P I R
      N E E
```

Answers on page 96.

A Trip to the Zoo!

Summer is a great time to visit the zoo and see lots of animals! What is your favorite animal to see at the zoo? Draw the animals you like best, and color their zoo home.

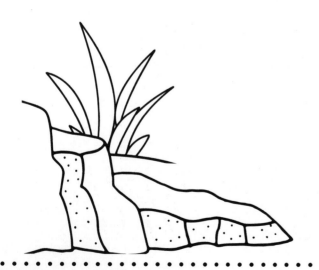

Animals and Their Babies

Can you help these animal babies find their parents? Color all of the animals, and draw a line between each baby animal and its parent. You can also cut out the animals and match them up, if you like.

Answers

Web Site *(page 14)*

Whose Kite Am I?
(page 24)
Ron, 2; Debra, 3; Pat, 1;
Jill, 4

Splish Splash
(page 36)

Mighty Monument *(page 42)*

Wild Wally's Water Park *(page 52)*

It's a Hot One Today *(page 65)*

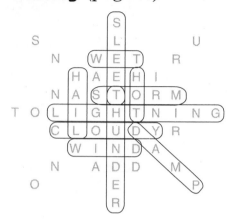

A Sunny Day Seek *(page 72)*

Fruit Salad *(page 93)*

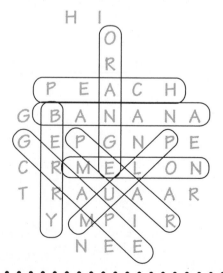